A Discourse Concerning Love

or

The More Excellent Way to Edify the Church of Christ:
the design of which is to revive that grace
(now under such decays) among
Protestants of all persuasions

by

Nathaniel Vincent, M.A.
Minister of the Gospel

"And above all things have fervent charity
among yourselves." 1 Peter 4:8

"Let your moderation be known unto all men;
the Lord is at hand." Philippians 4:5

"But if ye bite and devour one another, take heed ye
be not consumed one of another." Galatians 5:15

Edited by Rev. Don Kistler

Soli Deo Gloria Publications
. . . for instruction in righteousness . . .

Soli Deo Gloria
P.O. Box 451, Morgan, PA 15064
(412) 221-1901/FAX 221-1902

*

A Discourse Concerning Love was first published in London in 1684. This Soli Deo Gloria reprint, in which spelling, formatting, and grammar changes have been made, is ©1998 by Don Kistler and Soli Deo Gloria.

*

ISBN 1-57358-079-1

Contents

To the Reader

Although my name is in the mouths of many, and
tongues have scourged it most severely, and most false reports have been spread concerning me both in city and
country, yet I could more patiently have borne the killing
of my reputation if the honor of God had not been at all
concerned. A regard for His name and His gospel's credit
prevails with me to break silence; and love for others
makes me fear their being scandalized to their prejudice.
There is a design driven on by hell and Rome to introduce
atheism in order to advance popery, to make men really of
no religion, that they may not hesitate to profess themselves of the Romish perversion when they shall apprehend 'tis in their secular interest. Now because some
men's lives, by the grace of God, have been unblamable,
and tended to convince the world that there is a reality and
power in godliness, upon this account these persons are
singled out and loaded with calumnies and reproaches so
that, once they are represented as hypocrites, all religion
may the more easily be suspected as a cunningly devised
fable.

Let not those who have stupefied their own consciences
think that I have acted of late against mine. Though I
think I ought not to keep such a distance from the Church
of England as I did, yet I have no preferment in it, neither
can I submit to the terms of such preferment. Nay, I have
exceedingly hindered my own secular advantage by my
moderation, which is not the way to thrive in such a vio-
lent age as this. A moderate man is like one who parts two

who are fighting: instead of being thanked, he is liked by neither. He has blows from both for wishing them no worse a thing than peace.

From profane tongues I expected lies and slanders. That Master whom I serve met with no better treatment. He was called a wine-bibber, a friend to publicans and sinners; nay, said to have a devil. But though the slander is never so gross, it shall not hinder me from praying for the slanderer; and I hope I shall be enabled to live so that nobody shall believe him. If professors who are non-conformists speak against me and censure me as a temporizer, my answer is that with me it is a small thing to be judged of them, or of any man's judgment. My own conscience speaks another kind of language; and in that one I have a thousand witnesses of my integrity. God is convincing me of the vanity of popular applause, and how soon that kind of wind may turn and change. And if a conviction of this makes me more humble and low in my own eyes, dishonor will do me a far greater kindness than praise. I will say to humility, "O my safety and sweet ornament." And next to heaven, I expect the greatest rest for my soul in the exercise of this lovely virtue.

The fury of those who have been most enraged against me has but heightened my love for them. I have poured out more prayers and tears for them than they are aware of; and they will know what a true friend I have been to them when they come into another world. Those whose heads are hotter than their love shall not move my anger, but my pity and sorrow. And let them call me what they please, I shall own what is good in them, and requite their censures with supplications that their light and faith, their humility and love, may be increased, and that they may do nothing unbecoming the children of the God of love and peace;

nothing prejudicial to the church, or to themselves!

I have preached heretofore to multitudes while I was permitted. For all the churches in London, not being able to hold the tenth part of all the inhabitants, I thought they had better hear a doctrine agreeable to the Articles of the Church of England from my mouth than not hear at all. But it never was my practice to preach up a party; and it troubles me to see how much of religion is placed in smaller things, as appears by men's eagerness about them. What some thought a church, others thought a conventicle, like the ark of Noah, outside of which 'tis impossible to escape drowning in perdition. My design all along was to bring men to God by faith in Jesus, and that their hearts might be purified, and to persuade them to be holy in all manner of conversation. I confess I am somewhat altered from what I was; but it is in the extent of my love. But I am persuaded that this is an alteration for the better, and makes me more resemble Christ. Who can justly blame me for imitating the blessed Jesus, who loves all sincere Protestants of all persuasions, and has communion with them all! I add no more but that of the Apostle in Romans 15:7: "Wherefore receive ye one another, as Christ also received us to the glory of God."

Nathaniel Vincent

Chapter 1

The Church Is Like a Body

"Maketh increase of the body, unto the edifying
of itself in love." Ephesians 4:16

If I had a voice as loud as thunder, I would cry "Fire, Fire,"
with a wish that all England might hear. A flame is now kin-
dled much worse than that which burned down London. This
flame threatens both Church and State with ruin, and it is the
flame of fierce contention. Men's hearts are as hot as hell;
their tongues set on fire the course of nature. Such wrath,
such bitterness, such animosities everywhere appear, and
plainly show the body politic and body mystical are in a dangerous fermentation and fever, which I wish may not issue in
dissolution and destruction. That prediction of our Lord is
fulfilled: "Iniquity shall abound, and love shall wax cold"
(Matthew 24:12). Lust indeed breaks out into a flame; men's
passions are hot unto the highest degree, and fury makes
them abound in transgression.

But a deadly damp has seized on love. No wonder that the
Church's pulse beats in disorderly fashion; no wonder that
she is languishing and ready to die, for love is the cause of her
increase and edification.

Is there no balm in Gilead? Is there not a physician there?
Are the spots and symptoms such as show the disease to be
mortal, and that there is no remedy? Though the case is de-
plorable, it is not desperate. Were my text but minded, in it
might be found a sure recipe. Christ is the Church's Head

and healer; and were love revived, it would quickly bring His
body to a better and more healthy temper. Light may do
much, but love will do more. Love covers a multitude of sins;
love cures a multitude of maladies. The church increases and
edifies itself in love.

Though the Apostle was a prisoner, yet we find his heart
enlarged towards the Ephesians. Having before discoursed
concerning the mysteries of faith, in this chapter he presses
unity and love with the greatest vehemence. And in order
hereunto he exhorts to all lowliness and meekness. He knew
that pride was the cause of contention, and that humility and
love are the way both to the soul's and the Church's rest. He
uses great strength and cogency of argument that he may prevail. The saints are members of one body. They have been regenerated, and are acted upon by one Spirit, who has
effectually called them to a lively hope of one and the same
incorruptible inheritance. And in that inheritance there *is*
not, there *cannot* be, the least discord. They serve one Lord,
who is best served when His servants most agree together.
They are instructed in one gospel, justified by one faith, and
baptized in one name. Finally, this God is one God, who is a
most compassionate and indulgent Father to them all. And
from so many premises, how strongly and undeniably may we
conclude that all saints should be of one heart and one soul!

The Apostle, in thus preaching love and peace, showed he
had a very great regard to the glory of Christ the Head, who is
ascended far above all heavens that He might fill all things,
and that he had a great concern for His body, that being the
Church's edification. For, according to my text, it increases
and edifies itself in love.

In the words there are four propositions worthy of our observation:

1. The Church of Christ is compared to a body.

2. This body of Christ is imperfect in this world, and therefore should be continually increasing.

3. The body of Christ should diligently endeavor to edify itself.

4. The more love abounds among the members of the church, the more the whole body will be edified.

PROPOSITION 1. The Church of Christ is compared to a body. The Scripture often uses this metaphor of a body. Now a metaphor is a similitude in a word; and, indeed, there is a great resemblance between a human body and the Church of Christ, as by and by will be made evident. Believers are sometimes called the brethren of Christ (John 20:17), which intimates a very near relation. Sometimes they are called His spouse, whom He has betrothed to Himself forever (Hosea 2:19–20), and that's a relation much nearer, and signifies a more intimate and dear affection and familiarity. Sometimes they are called branches (John 15:1–4), and this expresses a nearer union still, and that both the life and fruitfulness of Christians depend upon their being and abiding in Christ, the true vine. Branches, though they grow, are without sense and feeling, so that neither they nor the vine feel any pain when they are cut or broken. Therefore, believers are called members; the church is called a body, and Christ is the Head, who is very much concerned both in it and for it. Christ is the Head of the church, and He is the Savior of the body. So Ephesians 3:6: "That the Gentiles should be fellow-heirs, and of the same body, and partakers of His promise in Christ by the gospel." Again, Colossians 1:18: "And He is the Head of the body, the church, who is the beginning and the firstborn from the dead, that in all things He might have the preeminence."

Zanchius takes notice of two things in these texts:

1. By the body we are to understand the true Church, the true mystical body of Christ. This church is made up of those who are really sanctified; of this body hypocrites are not members, for though such are visibly saints, yet in truth they are under the dominion of sin, and shall receive for their hypocrisy greater damnation. Though hypocrites profess themselves to be Christ's members, yet really they are not united to Him. Christ lives not, rules not, acts not in them, as He does in sincere Christians. Let them seem to be His followers, let them pretend never so highly to be His friends, yet really they are strangers of whom Christ will profess at the great day that He never knew them. Luke 13:26–27: "Then shall ye begin to say, 'We have eaten and drunk in Thy presence, and Thou hast taught in our streets.' But He shall say, 'I tell you, I know you not whence you are; depart from Me, all ye workers of iniquity.' "

2. By the Church we are to understand the church militant, that part of the body of Christ which is militant on earth, not which is triumphant in heaven. The church above needs not exhortations to grow and increase in knowledge and grace; it needs not the means of edification. Sermons of love are not to be preached there. Glorified saints have not the least sinful defect; they see God face to face, and Christ as He is. And their love for their Father and Redeemer is answerable to the sight they have, and as much as they are capable of. And being refined from all remainders of sin, they have become such lovely creatures that they cannot but love one another with a most pure and perfect love. 'Tis the Church of Christ on earth the Apostle speaks of; this is the body that is to be edified. And alas, in how many respects—how certainly in all respects—does it stand in need of edification.

In the handling of this proposition, I shall first of all show the great resemblance between the Church of Christ and a body; second, I shall show what kind of body the Church of Christ is; and, last, I shall make application.

I will first show the great resemblance between the Church of Christ and a body.

1. The life of the body depends upon its conjunction with the head. Christ is the Church's life, and the Church could no more live without Christ than a body could remain alive after the head was severed from it. Our Lord calls Himself "the Way, the Truth, and the Life" also (John 14:6). By His blood He frees His Church from the sentence of death and condemnation which sin had brought her under, and makes her spiritually alive by His quickening Spirit. So that the Church breathes after God, walks with Him, labors in His work and service, all of which are evidences of spiritual life. We read in 1 John 5:12: "He that hath the Son hath life, and he that hath not the Son hath not life." They who by faith receive the Lord Jesus are purified, are regenerated, and shall live forever; but as many as through unbelief reject Him remain dead in sin and doomed to hell. Union with Christ is a most necessary, a most happy union. The Church's life from this union has its beginning and continuance unto consummation.

2. The head has a mighty influence upon the body. There is a powerful influence from Christ upon His Church; and what good it does is done by virtue of this influence. He is said to be "exalted far above all heavens, that He might fill all things" (Ephesians 4:10). Whatever grace and strength and comfort are communicated to believers is really all from Christ. He fills ordinances with efficacy, mercies with sweetness, afflictions with light and usefulness, and souls with greater degrees of grace and holiness, out of that "all fullness that it has pleased the Father should dwell in Him" (Colossians 1:19). Our Lord tells His disciples that they must abide in Him, for separated from Him they can do nothing

(John 15:5). No wonder the Apostle professes that "Christ is all, and in all" (Colossians 3:11). Though the body, the Church, should be never so much increased, a deficiency in the Head, Christ, need not be feared. Neither is it indeed possible, for in Him there is all the fullness of the Godhead. And consequently His righteousness and grace must be sufficient for the whole.

3. The body has many members, and these members have different offices. The Church likewise has various members, and their different stations, relations, and callings diversify their work and duties. Yet the doing of these duties is both comely and advantageous; and the more everyone does his own work, the more all are benefited. In Romans 12:4–5 the Apostle tells us that "as we have many members in one body, and all members have not the same office, so we being many are one body in Christ." And from thence he infers that all should use the gifts they have received, which are differing according to the grace and good pleasure of God the Giver.

It would be unreasonable for the ear to attempt to speak like the tongue, or the hand to see like the eye. The several members have their uses and work proper to them. "All are not apostles, all are not prophets, all are not teachers, all are not governors" (1 Corinthians 12:29). There are many, indeed most in the church, who have need to be taught and governed; and those who think themselves wise enough to instruct and govern themselves, and so despise their spiritual guides, usually are the most ignorant and unruly, and hugely need the help and conduct of others. The members must abide in their place and calling—masters, servants, parents, children, husbands, wives, magistrates, subjects, pastors, people—doing their duties which the Scripture, in their several stations and relations, calls for.

4. The body is fitly joined; and thus fitly joined is the

Church of Christ. The word signifies that there is a congruous order among the members of Christ. Without order an army would be a rout and not an army; a kingdom would become a confused, self-destroying multitude. The Church's God is the "God of order, and not of confusion" (1 Corinthians 14:33). There is a rule for order and government, and a subordination in the Church; 'tis not a body of levellers: if there were a perfect parity, all would affect to rule, and none would care to be ruled. The reproof of two or three is more than the reproof of one; the Church's admonition and censure is still with greater authority. The flock is to submit themselves to their pastors "who are over them in the Lord" (Hebrews 13:17), and both pastors and people are to submit especially unto Christian magistrates, who are prophetically promised in the Old Testament that they should be nursing fathers to the church under the New. A right order in churches and families will have a mighty influence to make believers steadfast against temptations both to error and wickedness. The Apostle rejoiced in Colossians 2:5 when he "beheld their order, and the steadfastness of their faith in Christ."

5. The body is compact together, and so is the Church of Christ. The word used shows that the church is firmly knit unto Christ the Head, and the members one unto another. The hypostatic union between the natures of Christ shall never be dissolved, and neither shall the mystical union between Him and His members. And if this is so, then His true members must remain closely knit together. There are ligaments, joints, and bands whereby the body of Christ is held together. The spirit of grace and love unites the body to Christ, and members to members. The ministers of Christ are subservient unto this union, and ought to be preaching and commending love, which is a grace of a uniting nature. The Apostle had a concern for the Colossians, which he expressed

by a great internal conflict, and that which he wished so vehemently for was that their "hearts might be comforted, being knit together in love" (Colossians 2:1–2).

Where is the member of the natural body that grows weary of its fellowship and is willing to be cut off? The arms, the hands, the legs, and the feet are all desirous to keep their places; and nature makes them abhor to be severed. True grace makes the members of the Church dislike separation. As they believe so, they very well like, and are desirous of, the communion of saints. A very black mark is set upon those who are of a contrary inclination. 1 John 2:19: "They went out from us, but they were not of us; for if they had been of us, they would no doubt have continued with us; but they went out that they might be made manifest they were not all of us."

6. God has set the members in the body as it pleased Him; the different gifts and graces which are in the church of Christ, and the members of it, are according to God's will and pleasure. He bestows larger gifts upon some and less upon others; and yet those who have less are not useless. Some saints receive greater measures of grace, others smaller; but all have that grace which is true, and which at last will end in glory. Some members of the Church are higher, others lower, and yet they should not envy or despise one another, for God has assigned their place unto both; the higher may direct the lower, and the lower may serve the higher. "The eye cannot say to the hand, 'I have no need of thee'; nor the head to the feet, 'I have no need of you'; and those members of the body which seem to be more feeble are necessary" (1 Corinthians 12:21–22). By the grace of God the members of Christ are what they are. They have nothing but what they have received; and the more any have received, the more humble and diligent they should be; for where much is given, much will also be required.

7. In the body, nourishment is conveyed unto the parts, and the whole is hereby sustained. "The body of Christ also by joints and bands having nourishment ministered, and knit together, increaseth with the increase of God" (Colossians 2:19). The Church of Christ has food to eat which the world knows not of. It has spiritual senses, a spiritual appetite, and its food is spiritual. The Word of God is compared to food: here is milk for babes and stronger meat for more grown saints. No food is so profitable and nourishing, no food so pleasant, no food so necessary. Harken to the profession of Job 23:12: "Neither have I gone back from the commandment of His lips; I have esteemed the words of His mouth more than my necessary food." David cried out, "How sweet are Thy words unto my taste, yea, sweeter than honey to my mouth!" (Psalm 119:103). And the prophet Jeremiah speaks to the same purpose: "Thy words were found, and I did eat them, and Thy word was unto me the joy and rejoicing of my heart" (15:16).

The body of Christ is nourished by His Word, and other ordinances are appointed for the increase of this body. A famine of this Word deserves to be dreaded as a very sore judgment. The better the food, if it is well-digested, the better the nourishment and the purer the blood, and the body will be more prosperous and healthy. The more purely and sincerely the Word of God is dispensed, the more the members of Christ will become stronger, and the inward man will be the more renewed day by day. As Christ gives His Word, so He vouchsafes Himself to be food to His members. "My flesh is meat indeed, and My blood is drink indeed" (John 6:55). And by this they are nourished unto that life which is eternal. It might also be added that Christ is the clothing of His body as well as its nourishment. His righteousness is the robe which covers their guilt and nakedness. His grace beautifies and adorns His saints, and therefore they are bid "to put on the Lord Jesus Christ, and to make no provision for the flesh, to fulfill the lusts thereof" (Romans 13:14).

8. In the body, the members and parts are operative and active for the good of the whole. In the Church there is an *energeia*, an effectual working in the measure of every part, that the whole may be increased. The new nature which is in sincere believers inclines them unto action suitable to that nature; sloth is exceedingly opposite unto religion. God is a rewarder of them who diligently seek Him. To seek Him negligently is indeed to neglect Him.

The members of Christ are industriously to do their duty towards their Father, and their Head, and likewise towards one another. Hence it is that we read of the labor of love which the Apostle requires and encourages: "God is not unrighteous, to forget your work and labor of love which you have shown towards His name, in that you have ministered to the saints and do minister. And we desire that every one of you do show the same diligence to the full assurance of hope unto the end; that ye be not slothful, but followers of them who through faith and patience inherit the promises" (Hebrews 6:10–12).

The members of Christ's Church are to be active, but in their place and calling; for if they act irregularly, that action will be against the body and to its prejudice, not to its edification. Every part has its place, and that place it must keep, and not aspire higher without a call. That measure of grace which it has received, it must faithfully exercise with a regard to the Church's good as well as its own.

9. The whole body, as well as all its members, is animated by one soul; and the Church, with all its true members, is animated by one and the same Spirit. We read in Ephesians 4:4: "There is one body and one Spirit," and again in 1 Corinth-

ians 6:17: "He that is joined to the Lord is one Spirit." The same Spirit which is in the Head is in all the members who are joined to Him. And so the Apostle does not hesitate to say, "If any man have not the Spirit of Christ, he is none of His" (Romans 8:9). All that light which the members of Christ have is from the Spirit. He has caused a marvelous light to shine into their hearts, who before were under the power of darkness. He likewise is the worker of that liberty and ability which they have unto what is good. Before they had freedom, but it was only to do evil continually. These members of Christ are all changed into His image, which is their glory, but the beginning of that change, and the progress of it unto greater glory, are from and by the Spirit. 2 Corinthians 3: 17–18: "Where the Spirit of the Lord is, there is liberty. But we all, with open face, beholding as in a glass the glory of the Lord, are changed into the same image from glory to glory, even as by the Spirit of the Lord." The Spirit dwells in all true believers, and Christ has promised that He shall abide in them forever (John 14:16–17). Soul and body indeed may be separated, but the Spirit and the saint shall not.

The very bodies of believers are affirmed to be the temples of the Spirit where He dwells and abides. 1 Corinthians 6:19: "What, know ye not that your body is the temple of the Holy Ghost which is in you, which you have of God, and ye are not your own?" And if the body is His temple, surely the heart and soul should be, as it were, the *sanctum sanctorum*, the holiest of all—filled with light and grace that it may be also filled with peace and joy.

10. The body is under the soul's conduct and command; the Church is conducted and ruled by the Spirit of Christ. The eyes see, the ears hear, the hands work, and the feet move according to the soul's will and pleasure. And as it has *despoticum imperium*, the command and government of the

members, so it acts on them, and their operations are from the soul's presence. For if the soul were gone, the body would immediately become a clod of earth, and the members would be deprived of all strength and motion. The Spirit of Christ commands and acts upons His members. He makes them see the invisible God, and that world which is invisible. He makes them hear the voice of Christ so as to obey His call. He makes the hands holy, having first purified the heart, and employs them in working righteousness. He turns the feet into the way of God's testimonies, and strengthens believers so that they run and are not weary; they walk without fainting.

A Christian's conduct is called "walking in the Spirit" (Galatians 5:16). "This I say, then: walk in the Spirit," that is, in His light, in His strength, and according to His will, "and fulfill ye not the lusts of the flesh." Without this walking, 'tis a vain thing to pretend to be in Christ, or to hope for justification by His righteousness; for the Son of God was made a sacrifice for sin "that the righteousness of the law might be fulfilled in them, who walk not after the flesh but after the Spirit" (Romans 8:4). What kind of saints would there be, what exemplary members, what illustrious assemblies, if everyone had in a greater measure crucified the flesh with its lusts and affections, and had a more attentive and obedient ear to hear what the Spirit said unto the churches! You have seen, I trust, the resemblance between the Church of Christ and a body.

In the second place, I am to tell you what kind of body the Church of Christ is.

1. The church is a body of men. Ezekiel 34:31: " 'And ye My flock, the flock of My pasture, are men, and I am your God,' saith the Lord God." I grant the elect angels have Christ as their Head, but all the apostate ones were left in that

misery into which by sin they brought themselves. And
though the Son of God is the Lord and keeper of the holy
angels, yet He is not their Redeemer, as He is of His Church
for whom He died. When this Savior was born, the tongues of
angels proclaimed "peace on earth, goodwill towards men"
(Luke 2:14). Though the world lies in wickedness, yet the
Church is gathered out of the world. The saints themselves
were sometimes "dead in sins and trespasses; and walked
according to the course of this world, according to the prince
of the power of the air; fulfilling the desires of the flesh, and
of the mind; and were by nature the children of wrath, even
as others" (Ephesians 2:1–3).

All the stones of God's spiritual temple are dug out of the
common quarry of mankind; and, to keep them humble, they
should often look to the rock from whence they were hewn.
All the sons and daughters of the Lord almighty are of
Adam's lapsed race, without exception. The grace of God is
admirable in making a church of such as these. The body of
the first Adam was formed out of the dust, but the mystical
body of the second Adam was formed out of that which is a
great deal worse, a mere mass of corruption. And as there is
not a saint but was once a sinner, so those sinners who are
chosen and called and made faithful are not of the wise
commonly, or of the mighty, or noble of the world. "But God
hath chosen the foolish things of the world to confound the
wise; and God hath chosen the weak things of the world to
confound the things that are mighty; and base things of the
world, and things despised, hath God chosen, to bring to
nought things that are; that no flesh should glory in His presence; but according as it is written, 'He that glorieth, let him
glory in the Lord' " (1 Corinthians 1:27–31).

2. The Church is a body governed by the best laws. The
Lord Himself is their lawgiver; and He is holy, and just, and

good. And His commands are like Himself: "holy, just, and good also" (Romans 7:12).

There is a law of sin which the men of the world obey. This law commands what the law of God forbids, and forbids what the law of God commands. Darkness and light are not more contrary than these two laws are. But this law of sin is a law of death. Obedience is destructive to him who yields to it. The law of the Lord is quite of another nature: there is life and peace in the doing of it. Proverbs 7:2: "Keep My commandments and live, and My law as the apple of thine eye." Psalm 119:165: "Great peace have they that love Thy law, and nothing shall offend them." The more the church conforms to the laws of her Lord and Head, the more she recovers of the image of God which was lost by the fall, and partakes of the divine nature, escaping that corruption that lust causes in the world. This law is written in the heart which is changed and renewed; and the heart, being suited to the commandment, delights in obedience. Psalm 40:8: "I delight to do Thy will, O my God; yea, Thy law is within my heart." This law is of the highest authority, and therefore the saints should endeavor to keep it without fail. And whatever penalties they suffer, they will never have reason to repent of their faithfulness to their Lord, or their obedience to His precepts.

3. The Church is the wisest body and society in the world. Indeed, all the world besides is a company of mere fools and madmen. Are they not fools who hate knowledge? Are they not fools who join with Satan to undo themselves? Are they not fools who venture for a mere trifle, a little sinful gain or pleasure, to lose their precious souls, which are of more value than the whole world put together? Are they not fools who have salvation, life, and immortality offered to them, and neglect the offer? who are warned to flee from future wrath, and the vengeance of eternal fire, and yet will run there, and are

angry with any who endeavor to stop them? Oh, how has sin bereaved men of their wits and understandings!

But the Church of Christ is savingly enlightened, all her true members made wise unto salvation. They are so wise as to make their peace with God, believing in Jesus and relying on His blood for reconciliation. They are so wise as to follow the Lamb, and that path must be best and safest wherein He leads them. They are so wise as to make timely provision for eternity, and to commit the keeping of their souls into a strong hand which never lost any whom it undertook to keep and to secure. Therefore the Apostle speaks with so much confidence in 2 Timothy 1:12: "I know whom I have believed, and I am persuaded that He is able to keep that which I have committed to Him against that day." What is the wisdom of this world compared with the Church's wisdom, which is spiritual? The Apostle undervalues the policy of princes in comparison to the gospel; that policy comes to nothing, this gospel guides to glory. 1 Corinthians 2:6–7: "Howbeit we speak wisdom among them that are perfect; yet not the wisdom of this world, nor of princes of this world (who yet get most by their wisdom), that come to nothing: but we speak the wisdom of God in a mystery, even the hidden wisdom which God ordained before the world unto our glory."

4. The Church is a body of great beauty and excellency, called therefore in Song of Solomon 6:1 the "fairest among women." Zion is affirmed to be "the perfection of beauty" (Psalm 50:2). The Church is excellent in regard to her origin, for she is of heavenly extraction and born of God Himself. All her true members are new creatures; they are beautified with the image of God, and resemble Him in knowledge, righteousness, and true holiness. As sin is the greatest deformity, so holiness is the truest beauty; 'tis this which makes the angels shine. Nay, 'tis the glory of God Himself. Exodus 15:11:

"Who is like unto Thee, O Lord, among the gods? Who is like Thee, glorious in holiness?" How certain it is that the righteous man is more excellent than his neighbor. Now the Church is called "the generation of the righteous."

The Church is likened to a woman, because the woman exceeds the man in beauty; but she is such a woman as the like is not to be found. Revelation 12:1: "She is clothed with the sun, the moon is under her feet, and upon her head a crown," not of gold or diamonds, but better: "a crown of twelve stars." What can equal this glory of the Church? All flesh is grass, and all the glory of man as the flower of the field, which soon withers, and fades away. She is said to be clothed with the sun, because she is justified by Christ, the Sun of righteousness. The moon is said to be under her feet because all changeable things are below her spiritualized and raised affections. The twelve stars which are her crown signify the doctrine of the twelve apostles of the Lamb, whereby she is enlightened and brought at length to that light which is everlasting.

5. The Church is a body of great strength; for this body is strong in the Lord, and in the power of His might. Sinners are without strength—they can neither please God nor profit themselves—but the Church's members are strengthened with might by the Spirit in their inward man so that they can do things beyond the power of nature. They can see the invisible God; they can believe against hope; they can overcome and deny themselves; they can wrestle with the Almighty (and, as princes, they can prevail with Him); they can foil the principalities and powers of darkness; they can fight the good fight of faith; and they can lay hold of eternal life. All these are mighty acts indeed, too great to be performed by any who are hypocrites and ungodly.

The Church is most opposed, and yet is most victorious. It

will still abide in the world, notwithstanding all the world's rage—like the immortal regiment among the Persians that never was destroyed till the empire was destroyed; for if any soldier was killed, another presently was lifted up in his place. This bush of the Church is unconsumed in a flame; nay, it has been most green and flourishing when the flame has been fiercest. God has strengthened and preserved her; and her preservation may be looked upon as one of the greatest arguments and miracles of providence.

The Church is a body to whom the whole world is beholden. It should be the joy of the earth, for it is the security of the whole earth. How soon would the tares be plucked up, bound in bundles, and cast into the fire if it were not for the wheat which grows among them (Matthew 13:29)? The Church is a friend, and wishes well to mankind. It is her prayer that God's way may be known on earth, and His saving health among all nations; that the kingdoms of the world may become the kingdoms of the Lord, and of His Christ. And, like a mother, she is in travail for the conversion and salvation of a greater multitude of souls. Why should the world be angry and recompense evil for good? They should all be wise at length, and desire to be incorporated into the Church, and be resolved to go with her; for they may be well assured that God is with her (Zechariah 8:23).

7. The Church is a body that will at length, by many degrees, be made more glorious than 'tis at present. Now it is truly sanctified, it is highly dignified; but it does "not yet appear what it shall be" (1 John 3:2). But when Christ the Head shall appear the second time, without sin, unto salvation, what a glorious church will appear with Him (Colossians 3:4)! "Every member will shine as the sun in the Father's kingdom" (Matthew 13:43). And what a glorious spectacle will that be, to behold all the saints together in a company, and every one

of them shining forth as the sun, and the Son of God at the
head of them! How, with our cries and groans and serious
diligence in preparing for it, should we continually be hasten-
ing the coming of that day of God!

Christ's body, the Church, has its defects and blemishes
while it sojourns here below, but at the last day all the spots
will be off, all the wrinkles smoothed, and the end of Christ's
death will be fully attained. Now the Apostle tells us that He
gave Himself for His Church "that He might sanctify and
cleanse it, and present it to Himself a glorious Church, not
having spot or wrinkle, or any such thing; but that it should
be holy, and without blemish" (Ephesians 5:26–27). How gor-
geously appareled, how richly adorned, how amiable and
lovely will the Lamb's Bride at last be when Satan shall be
quite vanquished, death swallowed up in victory, and sin shall
cease to have a being! when light shall be without any darkness, joy without sorrow, purity without the least mixture of
defilement! When Christ puts the crown of life upon His
Church's head, then Song of Solomon 4:7 will be fully verified: "Thou art all fair, my love; there is no spot in thee."

Application

USE 1. Let the Church, and all the members of it, consider their relation unto Christ their Head, and do that duty
which such a relation calls for. They are Christ's and not
mammon's; they are Christ's and not their own; they are His
purchase, His spouse, nay, parts and pieces and members of
Him which He has bought and united to Himself. 'Tis highly
against all reason that they should seek to please themselves
in a sinful and self-destroying manner.

Their duty towards Christ, their Lord and Head, is in several particulars.

1. The members of Christ should love Him in great sincerity. The Apostle wishes that the grace of God may be with all such sincere lovers (Ephesians 6:24). Dissembled and seeming love is really none at all, and in several respects worse than none. Christ's love for His Church was most real. How exceedingly low was His humiliation that she might be advanced! How great were His sufferings for her eternal redemption! The Apostle speaks as one amazed at the height, length, depth, and breadth of Christ's love which passes knowledge (Ephesians 3:18–19). And if the Head is so full of love toward all the members, certainly the members will be in the worst sense unnatural if they return not love to their Head and Savior. They should prize Him most highly, counting all things but loss and dung that they may win Him (Philippians 3:8). They should mourn when He withdraws, but rejoice exceedingly when they enjoy His presence and see His face, who is altogether lovely. They should value His Word and ordinances, in which He is to be found, and delight themselves in the contemplation of His fullness, and that great and everlasting salvation whereof He is the Author. Their very souls should love Him (Song of Solomon 3:4), which expression intimates both the truth and the strength and fervency of affection. And truly our Lord is so excellent that there is no danger or possibility that love for Him should be excessive.

2. The members of Christ should endeavor to promote His honor and glory. They should be very zealous that their Head may be advanced and have the preeminence over all things. Their tongues should be showing forth His praises, commending Him to the world as the best of princes, as the only Savior, and declaring the unreasonableness of the world's prejudices against His yoke and burden, which are so easy and so light (Matthew 11:30). They should earnestly desire that Christ their Lord may be the world's universal

monarch, and that all earthly kings and emperors may cast down their crowns before Him and willingly submit to His scepter and government.

3. The members of Christ should obey all His commands. John 14:15: "If ye love Me, keep My commandments." And verse 21: "He that hath My commandments, and keepeth them, he it is that loveth Me." It is a monstrosity of nature if any of the members should not be placed under the Head. Surely, then, all the members of Christ should readily be subject to Him. Thus to be subject is to reign. Obedience is the great sacrifice to be offered according to the New Testament. The saints are called priests, and kings as well as priests, a royal priesthood (1 Peter 2:9). Therefore, to obey the Lord Jesus contains in it no less than a regal honor. He should be reverenced, and all His commands performed. He who hears Christ's sayings and does them is the wise builder whose house shall never fall. He is indeed the blessed man, and is in the right way to life and immortality. Revelation 22:14: "Blessed are they that do His commandments, that they may have right to the Tree of Life, and may enter in through the gates into the city."

4. The members of Christ should live by faith upon Him. They are to expect the remission of sin and deliverance from the wrath to come in no other way. When they have done their best and most, they must look unto Jesus that through Him they may be accepted; for there is no way to be accepted but in the Beloved (Ephesians 1:6). In all their temptations, sorrows, and sufferings they are to depend upon Him for succor, joy, and sufficient grace. The body is secured and, in spiritual warfare, has both conduct and conquest by acting out faith in Christ the Head. Every member therefore should imitate the Apostle, who said, "The life which I now live in the flesh, I live by the faith of the Son of God, who loved me, and

gave Himself for me" (Galatians 2:20).

5. The members of Christ should do nothing unbecoming His members. The glory and name of Christ, and the credit of the gospel, should be very dear to them; and they ought to be "blameless and harmless, without rebuke, in the midst of a crooked and perverse generation, and shine as lights in the world" (Philippians 2:15). They should manifest that they abide in Christ by walking as He walked. They should be patient, meek, and lowly as Christ was, condemn the world as He condemned it, count it their meat and drink to do the will of God as He did, and, since Christ endured the opposition of sinners against Himself, so should they. Though the foes of Christ are numerous, and oppose His interest with never so great force and fury, yet His members must never be ashamed to own their Head, nor afraid to follow Him. It becomes them, and it concerns them, to cleave to Him "with full purpose of heart" (Acts 11:23); for to leave Him is to be lost forever, and to bid farewell to blessedness and life eternal.

USE 2. Let the members of this body, the Church, consider the relation they have one to another. They are indeed very near, and should look upon themselves as very near one to another. And this relation should be of mighty efficacy to persuade them to perform those mutual duties which are incumbent upon them. In general, all particular members should consult the good of the whole Church. They believe in the holy catholic Church, and their love should run parallel with their faith—and care will be an effect of true love. A private spirit is very prejudicial to the body of Christ, for only one part is minded, and not another. It is just as if there should be an endeavor to make one member of the natural body great and strong, with no concern for how weak, feeble, and small the other members remain. It is lamentable that there are so many parties in the Christian church, but 'tis more to be lamented that these parties are so selfish, and so little mind the common interest; when this is neglected, their private interest cannot be regarded so truly as it should be. For if a whole town is burned to the ground, no particular house escapes the fury of the flames. No man's cabin can be secured if the ship is cast away and sinks to the bottom of the sea.

There are several counsels which I would entreat the members of the Church to follow, that it may be the better with the Church and with themselves:

1. Let not the higher members despise the lower. You who are higher, "what have you that you have not received? Why then should you glory, as if you had not received it?" (1 Corinthians 4:7). That's a Scripture whose sharp point should prick the bladder, and let out pride and self-conceitedness. Philippians 2:3: "Let nothing be done through strife or vain-glory; but in lowliness of mind let each esteem the other better than themselves." Moses, the holiest and most useful man in his time, was the meekest man upon earth (Numbers 12:3). As for the Apostle Paul, though he labored more abundantly than all the apostles to spread the gospel and faith of Christ, yet in what a humble style does he write of himself, and surely his heart and pen went together! 1 Corinthians 15:9: "I am the least of the apostles, that am not worthy to be called an apostle." Nay, he abases himself beneath all saints, as well as all apostles, and ventures the critic's scoff in coining the word *elachistotero*, to show how low he was in his own thoughts. Ephesians 3:8: "Unto me, who am less than the least of all saints, is this grace given, that I should preach among the Gentiles the unsearchable riches of Christ."

2. Let not the lower members of the Church be discon-

tent. Every member is highly favored, highly honored; every member is under the Head's care, and shall at last be fully happy in and with Christ Jesus. To be a doorkeeper in the house of God was looked upon as an honor and privilege by a king of Israel (Psalm 84:10). The least degree of true grace is of more worth than all the gold and silver that God has made. Saints are to be blamed when discontent because they are not of the highest rank; for all saints are children, all are heirs, all are firstborn. Therefore the Church is called "the Church of the firstborn" (Hebrews 12:23), nay, they are all, even the meanest of them, advanced to kingly dignity. Revelation 1: 5–6: "To Him that hath loved us, and washed us from our sins in His own blood, and hath made us kings and priests unto God and His Father, to Him be glory and dominion forever."

3. Let the members of the Church be sensible of the need in which they stand, one of another. How much are the higher members of the body beholden to the feet, which are the lowest of all! The body could not go without them, but only lame and crippled. God has ordered it so in His Church that, as the members are to have their main and principal dependence upon Christ their Head, so they are to have some kind of dependence upon one another. And the reason is that those two excellent graces of humility and love may flourish among them. Though the hand is fitly called the most useful member by philosophers, yet it cannot do everything. It cannot see like the eye, nor speak like the tongue; and if a man should attempt to go upon his hands, he would walk after a sorry and odd fashion. The strongest saints, nay, the ablest ministers are beholden to the meanest believers. The stronger are encouraged when the meaner do their duty. A word sometimes from a weak Christian may do much to edify a Christian more grown. The Apostle says he lived if the Thessalonians stood fast in the Lord (1 Thessalonians 3:8).

And a beggar could not beg more heartily for alms than he did for the prayers of the saints at Rome. Romans 15:30: "Now I beseech you, brethren, for the Lord Jesus Christ's sake, and for the love of the Spirit, that you strive together with me in your prayers to God for me."

4. Let the members of the Church "have the same care one for another that they have for themselves" (1 Corinthians 12:25). In the natural body it is thus: if the face is struck at, the arm endeavors to ward off the blow; if the body is in danger in one place, the feet are ready to carry it to a place of greater strength and safety. Christians should be concerned for their fellow Christians as for their fellow members. And mind more that instruction of the Apostle in 1 Corinthians 10:24: "Let no man seek his own" (that is, his own only), "but every man another's wealth."

5. Let the members of the Church sympathize with suffering members. We are commanded "to weep with those that weep" (Romans 12:15). The sorrows of afflicted Christians should be ours, and we should feel their burdens. 'Tis the glass eye that sheds no tears; 'tis the wooden arm and leg that feels nothing. Every member of Christ should be full of compassion. The injunction is plain, "Remember them that are in bonds as bound with them, and them which suffer adversity as being yourselves also in the body" (Hebrews 13:3). Those were upbraided, and threatened severely for their carnal security and hardness of heart, who were at ease when Zion was in trouble, and were not at all grieved for the afflictions of Joseph (Amos 6:6).

6. Let the members of the Church be concerned about fellow members who are sinfully distempered. If any part of the natural body ails in anything, all the other parts are ready to afford the utmost relief and assistance they are able. And why should Christians be careless of Christians, as if they were of

Cain's temper, who said, "Am I my brother's keeper?" If a beast is fallen we pity him, and are ready to help lift him up again; and should not a member of Christ who has fallen into sin and hurt himself so, by his fall, move our compassions? We are indeed carefully to avoid infection by those who are lapsed; yet 'tis our duty to "restore them in the spirit of meekness, considering ourselves, lest we also be tempted" (Galatians 6:1).

7. If one member of the Church is honored, all the members should rejoice with it. Is the hand envious at the eye's quickness? Or is the ear envious at the hand's activity? Envy is as unreasonable in the mystical body as in the natural body. We ought to rejoice in the gifts of others, and in their graces, and in their usefulness; else the Spirit of God who has given these gifts and graces, and has made them thus useful, will be grieved, and we shall hinder ourselves of that profit which we might reap from them.

8. Let there be no discord among the members of the Church, but they should perfectly agree together. By his Apologue concerning the unreasonableness of the members falling out with the body, Menenius Agrippa put an end to a contention that was likely to prove fatal between the Roman Senate and the common people. How unreasonable would it be that the hand should envy the eyes and endeavor to put them out? That the feet should take it amiss that they are lowest, and should fall kicking all the parts which are within their reach? Discord among saints is such a kind of unnatural and foolish contention. If Abraham, the father of the faithful, said unto Lot, "Let there be no strife between me and thee, for we be brethren" (Genesis 13:8), surely Christians should not argue or have strife with one another, "for we are members one of another" (Romans 12:5).

USE 3. Let the world take heed how they deal with the
Church, which is the body of Christ. It is Luther's observation
that if any part of the body is hurt and pained, the signs of
feeling appear in the head: the brows are contracted, the
tongue cries and the visage is altered. Christ the Head knows
all the sorrows of His Church; nay, in all her afflictions He is
afflicted. When Saul made havoc of the body on earth, the
Head in heaven cried out, as having felt his fury: "Saul, Saul,
why persecutest thou Me?" (Acts 9:4). Let the world be wise,
and the highest and greatest in it, for whatsoever injuries are
done to Christians for Christ's sake, He accounts them as
done to Himself. In hurting His body they strike Him where
He is most tender, most sensible; and such blows, if without
repentance, will be dreadfully avenged. Christ, who is the
Church's Head, is to be the world's Judge. And if when the
Lord comes with ten thousands of His saints hard speeches
shall be remembered, surely the world's hard usage of His
members shall not be forgotten, shall not pass unpunished. If,
at the great day, not feeding and clothing hungry and naked
saints will be punished with everlasting fire, oh, what a sin will
it be found to have taken away their food and raiment from
them! If Christ will be so angry with those who did not visit
believers in prison (Matthew 25:43), where shall they appear
who were the imprisoners of them! The world should not be
cruel to Christians, since Christ will quickly appear to judge
the world in righteousness. So much for the first proposition,
that the Church of Christ is compared to a body.

Chapter 2

The Body of Christ Is Imperfect

PROPOSITION 2. The body of Christ is imperfect in this world, and therefore continually should be increasing. Hence it is that Christians are exhorted to "grow in grace, and in the knowledge of our Lord Jesus Christ" (2 Peter 3:18), and not only to "be steadfast and unmovable," but "always to abound in the work of the Lord" (1 Corinthians 15:58).

In handling this proposition, I shall first show in what respects the Church of Christ here on earth is imperfect; second, in what sense the Church should be continually increasing; third, I shall produce several reasons for this increase of the Church; and last I shall give you the uses that may be made of it.

I begin with the first of these, and shall show in what respects the Church of Christ on earth is imperfect. Two things are here to be considered. First, the number of the Church's members is not yet completed. Second, those members who actually are of the Church are imperfect, the very best of them, as long as they remain in this world.

1. The number of the Church's members is not yet completed. There are more still to be called out of the world and brought home to Jesus. All are not gathered whom the Father has designed to give Him. John 10:16: "And other sheep I have, who are not of this fold; them also I must bring, and they shall hear My voice, and there shall be one fold, and one shepherd."

(1) Many, 'tis to be hoped, who have heard the gospel

27

shall be converted, though as yet they are not. Though they have hitherto resisted the Holy Ghost, yet at last they shall yield unto His call and striving. When the day of power and the time of love have come, they shall be made willing to receive a Savior, to be the Lord's, and to serve the Lord, though now never so great an obstinacy and unwillingness is displayed (Psalm 110:3).

(2) Many who are in the loins both of believers and unbelievers shall in due time be born, and be born again. The Church shall never quite be discontinued; it may indeed sometimes be less visible, but it always has a being. God will have a seed to serve Him in every future generation (Psalm 22:30).

(3) The natural branches are to be grafted in again to their own olive tree. Romans 11:24: "For if thou wert cut out of the olive tree which is wild by nature, and wert grafted contrary to nature into a good olive tree, how much more shall these (that is, the Israelites), which be the natural branches, be grafted into their own olive tree?" Blindness in part has happened to Israel, but they are still beloved for their Father's sake; and at length the veil which is upon their hearts shall be taken away, and they shall look unto Him whom their fathers crucified and be saved by Him. For He is the Messiah, the Deliverer who has "come out of Zion, and shall turn away ungodliness from Jacob" (Romans 11:26). Now when Israel shall be added to the Christian Church, how will this Church be increased! It will be a very glorious augmentation, like a resurrection from the dead. Romans 11:15: "For if the casting away of them be the reconciling of the world, what shall the receiving of them be but life from the dead?"

(4) The kingdoms of the world are to become the kingdoms of the Lord, and of His Christ (Revelation 11:15). I grant that this is in part already true: the Gentiles have been

preached to, and have obeyed the gospel. Christ, according to the Father's promise, has had the heathen given to Him for His inheritance, and some of the uttermost parts of the earth for His possession; but we may rationally conclude that, after the destruction of Antichrist, and the utter overthrow of his power and usurpation, many more kingdoms of the world will submit unto the Lord Jesus, and His Church hereby will have a vast increase. We find, in Revelation 18, Babylon destroyed, and the kings of the earth, and the merchants who committed fornication with her, crying, "Alas! Alas!" and lamenting her sudden and utter downfall. We see the heavens, and the holy apostles and prophets, rejoicing over her because God had avenged them upon her. And then it follows in Revelation 19:12 that upon the head of Christ were many crowns, which image shows the subjection of many kings to Him. And verse 6: "There is a voice of a great multitude, as the voice of many waters, and as the voice of mighty thunderings," as if all the world did join together in saying, "Alleluia, for the Lord God omnipotent reigneth." From all this it appears that the Church as yet is incomplete, and that greater numbers of converts are to be expected. And how should the promises of the Church's enlargement in the latter days be thought upon with joy, and how earnestly should we pray that those promises may be accomplished!

2. Those members who actually are of the Church are imperfect, the very best of them, as long as they remain in this world. How plainly does the wise man speak in Ecclesiastes 7:20: "There is not a just man upon the earth, that doeth good and sinneth not." There is many a just man upon earth; and every just man's practice is to do good. But there is not one who so does good as not to be chargeable with the least evil. The Apostle James, who is so much for joining good works with faith, yet acknowledges that in many things we all

offend (James 3:2). And the Apostle Paul, that great saint and preacher, speaks thus of himself (and surely he would not tell a lie through abundance of humility) in Philippians 3:12–14: "Not as though I had already attained, neither were already perfect . . . but forgetting the things which are behind and reaching forth to those things which are before, I press towards the mark for the prize of the high calling of God in Christ Jesus." The imperfection of the saints and members of the Church on earth will be evident in several respects.

(1) The knowledge of the saints is imperfect. He who knew as much as any says, "We know in part, and prophesy in part," and "now we see through a glass darkly" (1 Corinthians 13:9, 12). David, who was wiser than his enemies, who had more understanding than all his teachers, than the ancients, yet prays still that God would teach him, that God would open his eyes and give him understanding (Psalm 119), which expressions show a remainder of ignorance in him, a trouble at it, and a desire after a more perfect instruction.

(2) Holiness at present is imperfect in the best of men, as well as knowledge. Other graces cannot be perfect if knowledge is not. He who does not know the evil of sin as fully as he ought cannot hate it as much as he should. He who is imperfect in his knowledge of God and Christ must fall short in his faith and love, holy fear and reverence. There is not one sanctifying grace in us but needs further degrees. The Apostle makes it the constant work of believers here below to be cleansing themselves from all filthiness both of the flesh and spirit, and to be perfecting holiness in the fear of God (2 Corinthians 7:1).

(3) The victory over spiritual enemies is not yet fully obtained by militant saints. They are combatting, but they have not conquered; they resist Satan, and force him many times to flee, but he returns again and renews his assaults.

And although the God of peace has promised to tread him under their feet shortly, He has not yet done it (Romans 16:20). They have crucified the flesh with the affections and lusts; but though the flesh is fastened to the cross of Christ, and therefore the old man is said to be crucified with Him, yet the flesh struggles upon the cross. The body of sin is not quite destroyed, and some fleshly and worldly lusts and affections are stirring which are not totally mortified. Militant saints are not yet complete conquerors, for their enemies still make headway and continue the war, though at length they shall be made more than conquerors through Him who loved them (Romans 8:37).

(4) The joys of believers also are imperfect. All tears shall at last be wiped away from their eyes, but at present their eyes are full of them. The world's wickedness, and folly in that wickedness; professors' degeneracy; the Church's divisions, distresses, and corruptions; the dreadful tokens and signs of God's displeasure, if not of His departing; and finally their own spiritual distempers, which are so far from being perfectly cured—alas! these are enough to hinder their joy from being perfect.

(5) Their happiness is as yet but an imperfect happiness. All the world is miserable besides, and the saints are the only happy ones; and yet these, by many degrees, are not so happy as they shall be. This sad effect sin has by coming into the world: that not a man, not the *best* man can be fully happy till he is out of the world. The Church's true members are happy indeed, because God is theirs (Psalm 144:15), because Christ is theirs; but they must be happy only in part because God and Christ are but in part enjoyed.

In the second place, I am to show in what sense the Church should be continually increasing.

1. The Church should endeavor to increase in numbers, that the stone cut out without hands may become a great mountain and fill the whole earth (Daniel 2:34–35). 'Tis the world's misery that it hates and keeps its distance from the Church of Christ. But if this world were but taken into the Church, and were brought to believe in the same Jehovah, in the same Jesus, and to yield subjection to the same gospel, what a new and happy world would there be presently! This increase of the Church in numbers is to be endeavored in several ways.

(1) Prayer should be constant and very fervent for this increase. All the sons and daughters of Zion should be importunate that the city of God may be enlarged, that the Church may not have a barren womb or dry breasts; but that by reason of her numerous offspring she may enlarge the place of her tent, and without sparing she may lengthen her cords, strengthen her stakes, and stretch forth the curtains of her habitation (Isaiah 54:2). There is mercy enough in God, though the miserable sinners who come to Him are never so great a multitude. The fullness of Christ is so infinitely unmeasurable that 'tis sufficient to supply and to enrich the whole empty and beggared race of Adam. Heaven is of a capacity to contain millions of inhabitants more. Let us therefore pray that the conversion of souls may be by thousands, and that they may fly as a cloud and as doves to their windows (Isaiah 60:8).

(2) The promises of the Church's increase are to be believed and pleaded. In what a strain does God speak unto His Church! What promises does He make to her! Isaiah 60:3–5: "The Gentiles shall come to thy light, and kings to the brightness of thy rising. Lift up thine eyes round about, and see; all they gather themselves together, they come to thee. Thy sons shall come from far, and thy daughters shall be

nursed at thy side. Then shalt thou see, and flow together, and thy heart shall fear and be enlarged. Because the abundance of the sea shall be converted unto thee, the forces of the Gentiles shall come to thee." And verse 11: "Thy gates shall be open continually; they shall not be shut day nor night," that still there may be greater confluence. And verse 16: "Thou shalt also suck the milk of the Gentiles, and shalt suck the breasts of kings; and thou shalt know that I the Lord am thy Savior and thy Redeemer, the Mighty One of Jacob." These and such like promises are certain; that God who has made them is easily able to make them good. His glory and name, and His Son's honor, are much concerned in fulfilling them. And He is delighted to see His saints desirous, with respect to His name, that these promises may be performed.

(3) The Church is to be increased by the powerful preaching of the gospel. This preaching by all means is to be encouraged, for "faith comes by hearing, and hearing by the Word of God" (Romans 10:17). Those who preach Christ most and themselves least are likeliest to enlarge the Church of God. Those who are most skillful to convince men of sin, who are wise to win souls, who know Christ themselves and how to reveal Him to others, and with greatest zeal press the love and practice of holiness, are the pastors after the heart of God, and are likely to do as Jacob did to Laban, vastly to increase the flock of Christ. The Apostle was so far from hindering the preaching of the gospel that he was glad it was preached by those who did not preach sincerely. Surely the Church may have some benefit and enlargement by such. Philippians 1:15–18: "Some preach Christ even of envy and strife, and others also of good will. The one preach Christ of contention, not sincerely, supposing to add affliction to my bonds, but the other of love, knowing that I am set for the defense of the gospel. What then? Notwithstanding every way,

whether in pretense or in truth, Christ is preached; and therein I do rejoice, yea, and will rejoice."

(4) The avoiding of scandal does much for the Church's increase. The scandalous and loose lives of professors make the world conclude that the gospel is but a cunningly devised fable, and this hardens men in irreligion, and a profane contempt of God and Jesus Christ whom He has sent. The evil works of such as are called Christians for many of these latter ages has been a great impediment to the spreading of Christianity. Our Lord says, "Woe to the world because of offenses" (Matthew 18:7), for the world hereby is confirmed in prejudice and wickedness, and at last is more certainly ruined. But when the members of the Church work out their own salvation with fear and trembling, and show a vehement desire after the world's salvation also, this is the way to gain the world to Christ, and to turn it unto righteousness.

(5) The Church is mightily increased by the exemplary conduct of her members. When believers are zealous of good works, and without rebuke and blame; when they are patterns of piety, justice, mercy, meekness, patience, and self-denial; when they go about doing good, and by the heavenliness of their discourse and carriage declare plainly that they seek a better country than is to be found in this world, hereby they adorn the gospel, and render it more lovely in the world's eye, and more likely to be entertained. The ignorance of wicked and foolish men is silenced by well-doing (1 Peter 2:15), nay, they are forced to a confession that God is truly in His Church, and may at length consent and desire to be members of that Church where there is so much of God, and of His visible and apparent presence.

2. As the Church should increase in numbers, so all the members of the Church should strive to increase more and more in grace and goodness. They should strongly be in-

duced to this because of their own imperfection in grace, which imperfection fills them many times with inward trouble and tormenting doubts and fears, and makes outward affliction highly necessary. Besides, holiness is of such an excellent nature, and so perfecting of the nature of man, that the strongest desires for it are to be justified, and the most diligent endeavors after it to be commended.

Grace is increased in the members of Christ in several ways:

(1) It is increased by a serious and frequent engaging in those ordinances which He has instituted. He who has instituted these has promised blessing with them and adds the efficacy. Prayer, fasting, giving of thanks, receiving the Supper of the Lord, attending upon the Word preached, searching the Scriptures, and the like means of grace, when seriously used, exceedingly promote the growth of a Christian, making him become strong in spirit. The Church is the garden of God: the saints are planted there; the Word and ordinances of Christ are like the showers from heaven, and the husbandman's pains, which make these plants thrive and flourish. Psalm 92:13: "Those that be planted in the house of the Lord shall flourish in the courts of our God." But still it must be remembered that, though means are to be used, yet we must look beyond them unto Him who has appointed them, else they will never attain their end. 1 Corinthians 3:7: "So then neither is he that planteth anything, nor he that watereth, but God that giveth the increase."

(2) Grace is increased by the improving of providence. The dispensations of providence were various towards David; he was exercised with great severity, and likewise with great goodness. We read in Psalm 116:3: "The sorrows of death compassed him, and the pains of hell got hold upon him; he found trouble and sorrow." And in verse 10, he was greatly af-

flicted, and in this distress he called upon that God who is
merciful and gracious for deliverance, and his calling was
heard and his soul was delivered from death, his eyes from
tears, and his feet from falling. And now how is his heart affected and his graces strengthened! He is filled with love; he
is resolved to give himself to prayer as long as he lives; his soul
is at rest in God who has dealt bountifully with him; he offers
the sacrifice of thanksgiving, and he cries out, "Oh, Lord, I
am Thy servant, truly I am Thy servant" (verse 16), which is as
if he should say, "Lord! Thou art a master beyond all comparison; and as it is my firm resolution, so 'tis my happiness and
honor, as well as duty, to be a servant to Thee."

(3) The covenant of grace is to be studied, and the
promises applied, in order for a Christian to increase. God
has assured His people that He will perfect that which concerns them, and that He will not forsake the work of His own
hands. He has said that His servants shall "spring up as among
the grass, and as willows by the water courses" (Isaiah 44:4);
that "the righteous shall hold on his way, and they that have
clean hands shall wax stronger and stronger" (Job 17:9); that
"they shall bring forth fruit even in old age, and even then be
flourishing," and this shall be to show that "the Lord is upright" (Psalm 92:14–15). Such promises being prized and applied will make the new creature full of vigor, and perseverance will be certain. Harken to the Apostle in Philippians 1:
6–7: "Being confident of this very thing, that He who hath be-
gun a good work in you will perform it unto the day of Jesus
Christ, even as it is meet for me to think this of you all."

(4) Grace is increased by having recourse unto that
fullness which dwells in Christ. Therefore, growing in grace
and growing in the knowledge of Christ are joined together;
for Christ is full of grace and truth, and out of His fullness,
says John, "we all have received, and grace for grace" (John

1:16), aye, that is, grace answerable to that grace which is in Him. Grace is His purchase. He has it in possession. He gives it to all who have it, and every new degree is from the same hand. He is the object, the author, and the finisher of faith (Hebrews 12:2). They are the most growing and established saints who are least taken with the world, who have least confidence in themselves, who best understand and most look unto Jesus.

(5) All impediments of increase must be carefully shunned, such as pride, sloth, earthliness, or carnal and corrupt affections. If these, or things of like nature, prevail, they will prove to be to the soul what diseases are to the body, and make the members of Christ feeble and languish, depriving them both of their strength and beauty. These are sinful dispositions which must be purged if we would have our souls be healthy and prosperous. These are like weights which must be laid aside if we will run the race that is set before us, so as to obtain the prize (Hebrews 12:1).

In the third place, I am to produce several reasons why the Church should be continually increasing:

1. This increase is for the Father's glory. The more saints there are, the more God is honored; and the more any are saints, He has still the more glory from them. As the members of Christ grow stronger, their faith in God is firmer; their fear more filial, they love Him more with their heart, soul, and strength; they walk more humbly with Him. All this shows what right apprehensions they have of Him, and that they glorify Him as God, believing His presence, power, mercy, truth, and righteousness. That our Lord might persuade us unto fruitfulness and increase, He says in John 15:8: "Herein is My Father glorified, that ye bear much fruit; so shall ye be My disciples."

2. This increase of the Church is for the honor of Christ, the Church's Head. The largeness of a dominion and the multitude of subjects is the honor of a prince. The more sincere Christians there are, the kingdom of our Lord is the more enlarged, and He Himself is magnified the more. The Redeemer is glorified when the everlasting gospel goes forth; when His Word, which is the scepter of His kingdom, is believed and obeyed; when souls by whole multitudes come flocking to Him to be justified by His blood, sanctified and healed by His grace, and saved to the uttermost. How was Christ honored when after the first ten persecutions the Roman Empire submitted to the faith, the eagle gave way to the cross, and Constantine the Great threw down his crown at the feet of the Lamb of God. Then was that Scripture signally fulfilled, though a further accomplishment is still to be expected from Isaiah 55:5: "Behold, thou shalt call a nation that thou knowest not, and nations that knew not thee shall run unto thee, because of the Lord thy God, and for the Holy One of Israel, for He hath glorified thee."

3. In this increase of the Church, the operation of the Spirit is very illustrious. He wrought the miracles for the confirmation of the gospel, and made it at first to be entertained in the world. Wherever there is true faith, it is of His bestowing. Those who are regenerated are said to be born of the Spirit (John 3:6). The renewing of a soul is of the Holy Ghost (Titus 3:5). All spiritual gifts, all true grace, all solid comforts are from the Spirit. The more therefore light is spread, the more broadly gifts are distributed, the more plentiful communication there is of grace, the more peace and joy abound, the greater is the Spirit's glory. The Nicene Creed calls the Spirit "the Lord and Giver of life." As many members as Christ has, so many miracles there are of the Spirit's working, for He has raised them all to life who were once dead in sins and

trespasses as well as others.

4. This increase is for the Church's advantage; therefore it should be pursued. 'Tis a matter of joy and praise to saints to behold sinners converted and sanctified, to see prodigals coming to themselves, and coming home to their Father's house; to see strangers and foreigners made fellow-citizens with the saints, and of the household of God (Ephesians 2:19). And when these saints perceive that more light is imparted to them, and that they are filled fuller with the fruits of righteousness which are by Jesus Christ, to the glory and praise of God, they must apprehend this to be for their profit, if the truest riches may be called "gains," and pearls of the greatest price are of any value.

5. The world benefits by the Church's increase. Not a soul is gathered out of the world but something is secured of greater value than the world. If a city were on fire and burning quickly to the ground, the more persons are saved, the more goods are secured, the greater kindness is done to that city, because these persons and these goods escape the fury of the flames. Sin is ruining the world quickly, but all who in time come out from the world and touch not the unclean thing, and are incorporated into the Church of Christ, are safe as in a sanctuary, shall be delivered from the common destruction, and shall escape the vengeance of eternal fire in which all the wicked must burn forever.

6. The angels themselves are concerned with the increase of the Church. The apostate ones are confounded when, by all their subtlety and strength, they are not able to hinder the increase of Christ's government; nay, they are so overruled that they are made to promote His kingdom by those very means which were designed to overthrow it. And the elect angels are depicted as rejoicing at the repentance and conversion of a sinner. Luke 15:10: "Likewise I say unto you, there is

joy in the presence of the angels of God over one sinner that
repenteth." And if they are so glad at the conversion of one,
what an addition would it be to their joy to behold thousands
and millions added to the Church of Christ! 'Tis pleasing to
the angels to behold peace on earth, and God's goodwill ex-
pressing itself in the salvation of men (Luke 2:14), and upon
this account they cry, "Glory be to God in the highest."

Application

USE 1: of reproof to those who hinder the Church's increase. The furtherers of it I am sure are few, and the hinder-
ers many; therefore the more are concerned in the reprehen-
sion.

1. Enemies without endeavor, with might and determina-
tion to hinder the increase of the body of Christ; they hate
the light, and would fain hinder it from shining. They are
grieved that Jesus is preached, and are angry as well as
grieved; for they are unwilling that His subjects should become numerous. The world upon this account raises persecution; and how many at such a time fall away (Matthew 13:21)!
Cyprian laments the pressure of that persecution which had
so woefully wasted the flock he was over, and says that many
were ruined, the rest feared, the church languished, and few
stood against so furious an assault. We have large martyrolo-
gies, but if all apostates were registered how vast would be the
catalogues of them! 'Tis well that tribulation lasts but ten
days, a short time, else the world might tread the Church under. But the world's rage is without reason against the Church
of Christ, which will do no harm and desires to do the world
the greatest kindness.

2. Hypocrites within are to be reproved, for they hinder
the Church's increase. They are fitly compared to vipers,

which are said to eat the bowels in which they were bred. Our
Lord's anger is very hot, and His words sharp, against hypocrites. Matthew 23:13: "For they shut up the kingdom of
heaven against men; they refuse to go in themselves, neither
suffer they them that are entering to go in." They profess
high, but when they fall and notoriously reveal their un-
soundness, they wound the reputation of religion to the
Church's grief and disadvantage, and cause the hardening of
the ungodly in their wickedness—their convictions hereby being quite thoroughly extinguished.

3. The Church's increase is likewise hindered by impru-
dent members. Such are not so careful to avoid appearances
of evil themselves, and they blaze abroad the infirmities of
others, which infirmities love should find a mantle to cover.
Nay, many times they hear and report the most errant lies and
slanders whereby not only the person slandered suffers, but
likewise religion and the Church. These fools deserve to be
lashed severely for their inconsiderate talkativeness and un-
circumspect walking. And they should remember that the disciples of Christ are to be "wise as serpents and harmless as
doves" (Matthew 10:16).

4. Erroneous members and church-dividers are deeply
guilty of hindering the increase of the Church. Error has a
natural tendency toward division, for they who speak perverse
things endeavor to draw away disciples after them (Acts
20:30). And division is a grand impediment to edification.
The Church of Christ, after the giving of the Spirit on the day
of Pentecost, grew exceedingly. And one reason was that the
"multitude of them that believed were of one heart and of
one soul" (Acts 4:32). But division weakens the Church's
strength, and turns her own members against her by turning
them against one another. The Apostle severely rebuked the
Corinthians upon this score in 1 Corinthians 3:3: "For ye are

yet carnal; for whereas there is among you envying, and strife, and divisions, are ye not carnal, and walk as men?" It is as if he had said, "This unpeaceable and dividing temper makes you act not like members of Christ, but like men of the world, whom Christ bids His disciples to beware of as enemies to His interest and kingdom." Indeed, the corruptions of others are not to be approved, yet what is good and sound is to be owned; and we are to be taken with the image of Christ in whomsoever we see it shining.

5. Slothful, unfaithful, proud, and selfish pastors deserve as sharp a rebuke as any, because the Church's increase is hindered by their poor witness. Such seek their own things, not the things of Christ; their own profit, not the profit of many that they may be saved. 'Tis ordinary with them to "make the heart of the righteous sad, whom God has not made sad, and to strengthen the hands of the wicked, that he should not return from his wicked way, by promising him life" (Ezekiel 13:22). The Prophet prophecied sharply against the shepherds of Israel in Ezekiel 34:2–4: "Woe to the shepherds of Israel who feed themselves, not the flock. The diseased have ye not strengthened, neither have ye healed that which was sick, neither have ye bound up that which was broken, neither have ye brought again that which was driven away, neither have ye sought that which was lost. But with force and with cruelty have ye ruled them." Now if the flock is thus neglected, 'tis likely to be lessened, and the Church to be brought very low. Oh, what a dreadful account will such pastors have to give both of themselves and of the flock unto the Great Shepherd at the last day!

USE 2: of encouragement unto the Church of Christ notwithstanding her imperfection. Her spirit should not sink into despondency because perfection is not yet attained; but several truths may be offered as grounds of support.

1. That righteousness which is imputed to the Church of Christ is perfect. Though their faith, though their evangelical obedience is imperfect, yet the righteousness of Christ which their faith lays hold on is in every way complete. The obedience of one, that is, the Son of God, is sufficient to make many righteous, though never so many believe (Romans 5:19). "By one offering He hath perfected forever them that are sanctified" (Hebrews 10:14). The Apostle indeed is ashamed of his own righteousness, and afraid to be found in it, and desires to be found in Christ that he might have on that righteousness which is of God by faith. The obedience and sufferings of Christ are the righteousness imputed to them who believe; and 'tis called the righteousness of God because God contrived it and accepts it. Christ, who obeyed and suffered, is not only man, but above all God blessed forever. Christ has done and suffered enough to satisfy divine justice, to ransom and save souls, and to obtain eternal redemption for us. And here is a firm ground for the Church's consolation.

2. The sins of the Church's members are all pardoned; not so much as one is unforgiven. Colossians 2:13: "Having forgiven you all trespasses." Psalm 103:12: "As far as the east is from the west, so far hath He removed all our transgressions from us." The Church is espoused to Christ, and He has satisfied the law and justice for all her offenses. It may joyfully be said, therefore, "There is no condemnation to them that are in Christ Jesus" (Romans 8:1). Her Head and Husband having paid the Church's debts, payment from her is not expected and shall not be demanded.

3. Though the Church's members are imperfect, yet the least degree of true grace shall be owned. The smallest stars are stars, and are fixed in heaven as well as the greatest. The

weakest saints are saints, and as such shall be regarded. 'Tis
said of Christ, "He shall feed His flock like a shepherd; He
shall gather the lambs with His arm, and carry them in His
bosom" (Isaiah 40:11). The feeblest of Christians stand in
need of cherishing, and they shall have what they need. Our
Lord "will not break the bruised reed, nor quench the smok-
ing flax, until He sends forth judgment unto victory"
(Matthew 12:20).

4. The Church of Christ, notwithstanding her imperfection, is in a safer state than Adam was in innocence. The
union between his Creator and him was not so indissoluble as
the union between Christ and true believers. Life was
promised to him upon condition of his perseverance in obedience, but he had not a promise of grace to make him perse-
vere. But the saints have such a promise. God has said that He
will put His fear in their hearts, that they shall not depart
from Him (Jeremiah 32:40); that He will "strengthen and uphold them with the right hand of His righteousness" (Isaiah
41:10); that none shall pluck them out of the hand of Christ,
nor out of the Father's hand, "who is greater than all" (John
10:28–29); that nothing shall be able to separate them from
the love of God which is in Christ Jesus their Lord (Romans
8:39). Adam was entrusted with a treasure in his own keeping;
but he lost it, and ruined himself and his whole progeny.
Believers, therefore, are not thus trusted; both they and their
treasure are in the hands of Him who is able to save to the uttermost; and so both are secured. Their life is hidden with
Christ in God (Colossians 3:3).

USE 3: of advice to the Church of Christ, and all her true
members.

1. Let their imperfection keep them humble. There is not
a soul without a stain, nor a grace without a mixture, nor a

duty without a failing, nor a saint without some sin remaining. All therefore, nay, the very best of all, have reason to be low in their own eyes. The more humble we are, the more our hearts are suited to our present imperfect state, and the more of God's reviving presence, notwithstanding our imperfection, will be vouchsafed. "For, thus saith the high and lofty One, who inhabiteth eternity, whose name is holy, 'I dwell in the high and holy place; with him also that is of a contrite and humble spirit, to revive the spirit of the humble, and to revive the heart of the contrite ones' " (Isaiah 57:15).

2. Let the Church's members hunger and thirst after a greater measure of righteousness. Those who do so are blessed, "for they shall be filled," says He in whom all fullness dwells (Matthew 5:6). This is a hunger that is truly sacred, that never ends in starving, but in satisfaction. We should long more for the waters of life; the soul should thirst more vehemently for the living God, desiring to behold His glory, and to be changed more fully into His glorious image. Such kinds of desires widen the soul's capacity, and make it meet for a larger participation in both grace and comfort.

3. Let the Church believe in and long for that enlargement and glory that is promised in the latter days; but especially to be translated unto those mansions above, which her Head has gone to prepare for her. Let her long that her warfare may be well accomplished, her course faithfully finished, and the Crown of Life and righteousness received. And, to this end, let all her members tear the air and pierce the heavens with their cries: "Come Lord Jesus, come quickly" (Revelation 22:20). So much for the second proposition, that the body of Christ is imperfect in this world, and therefore continually should be increasing.

Chapter 3

The Body of Christ Should Diligently
Endeavor to Edify Itself

PROPOSITION 3. The body of Christ should diligently endeavor to edify itself. Before the Apostle had used the metaphor of a body; now he uses another metaphor, that of an edifice or building. The church is to edify itself, but the power to do this is from God; and her Lord, who empowers and strengthens her in this action, lays a just claim to all the glory. The Church is an edifice or a house, but a spiritual one; and therefore it is called a temple. Ephesians 2:21–22: "In whom (that is, Christ) all the building, fitly framed together, groweth unto a holy temple in the Lord; in whom you also are builded together for a habitation of God through the Spirit." This temple is holy, for God has set apart such as are godly for Himself. The stones are lively, for all saints are quickened to live to God and act for Him. In this temple sacrifices are offered, but they are spiritual: prayers, praises, other duties, and the heart of him who performs them. And though these sacrifices are never so spiritual, yet they are not accepted upon their own account, but are "acceptable unto God through Jesus Christ" (1 Peter 2:5).

In further handling this proposition, I shall first show upon what foundation the Church is to edify itself; second, show the end goal of this edification; and, last, make application.

In the first place, I am to show upon what foundation the

Church is to edify itself.

1. The knowledge of God is called a foundation. 2 Timothy 2:19: "Nevertheless the foundation of God standeth sure, having this seal, 'the Lord knoweth them that are His.' " God has, from eternity, foreknown and chosen His Church in Christ, that she should be holy and without blame before Him in love (Ephesians 1:4). This is a foundation laid before the foundation of the world, and will endure infinitely longer than the world shall. The Church's members should give all diligence to make their calling and election sure; for if they do these things they shall never fall, but an abundant entrance shall be administered to them into the everlasting kingdom (2 Peter 1:10–11). Now election is made sure by hearkening to, and obeying the call of, the gospel and departing from iniquity.

2. Christ the Rock is called a foundation in 1 Corinthians 3:11. "Other foundation can no man lay than that is laid, which is Jesus Christ." Though He was set at nought by the Jewish builders, yet He is the head stone of the corner; neither is there salvation in any other. The Church's faith must be firmer in Christ, her hope in Him more and more abundant; and she may build without fear, for the foundation will never fail the superstructure.

3. The doctrine of the apostles and prophets is also called a foundation (Ephesians 2:20). Both were inspired by the Holy Ghost, and the harmony and agreement between apostles and prophets, between the Old Testament and the New, makes the foundation more sure. The Church, that she may edify herself, is to eye the Scripture; then she will build according to the right rule. Unwritten traditions, that would impose upon her faith what the Scripture has not revealed, are to be rejected; and that light within that would lead her away from the written Word is no more to be followed than a

foolish night-fire. If she has Scripture for her faith and practice, she has good ground for both; and both may be justified before the Judge of all the world.

4. Obedience and good works are called a foundation. 1 Timothy 6:19: "Laying up in store for themselves a good foundation against the time to come, that they may lay hold on eternal life." This is done by doing good, by being rich in good works. Though good works are not meritorious (for eternal life is the gift of God), yet they are necessary to evidence our faith, and that the promises may be fulfilled. Glory and immortality are promised to those who, by patient continuance in well-doing, seek for them (Romans 2:7). He builds firm who builds his house upon a rock; and he builds thus who hears the words of Christ and does them. But he who hears and does them not is a foolish man, and builds his house upon the sand; and when the rain descends and the winds blow, and the floods come and beat upon his house, it will fall, and great will be the fall of it (Matthew 7:24–27).

In the second place, I am to tell you what the end goal of this edification of the Church must be.

1. The Church must edify itself that it may grow stronger. The stronger her faith is, the more will she glorify that God in whom she believes. In Romans 4:20 'tis said of Abraham, "He staggered not at the promise of God through unbelief, but was strong in faith, giving glory to God." The stronger her love, the more it will constrain her to labor in her Lord's work, and cast out the fear of suffering for His sake; for a strong love is stronger than death, and has a most vehement flame. Many waters cannot quench it, neither can the floods drown it (Song of Solomon 8:6–7).

2. The Church must edify itself that it may become larger. Prayer should be instant and constant, and pains should be

taken both by pastors and people, and godliness should be both in form and power, so that the "mountain of the house of the Lord may be established in the top of the mountains, and exalted above the hills, and all nations may flow unto it" (Isaiah 2:2).

3. The Church must edify itself that it may become more beautiful and glorious. The great day of the Church's public marriage to the Lamb is approaching. How careful should she be to cleanse and adorn herself that she may be found by Him in peace, without spot, and blameless (2 Peter 3:14). This beauty and glory which the Church is to endeavor after, and to long and hope for, you have described in Revelation 21:9–23: " 'Come hither, and I will show thee the Bride, the Lamb's wife.' And he carried me away in the Spirit to a great and high mountain, and showed me that great city, the holy Jerusalem, descending out of heaven from God, having the glory of God; and her light was like unto a stone most precious, even like a jasper stone, clear as crystal. The walls were high, the twelve gates were all pearls, the street of the city was pure gold, as if it were transparent glass. And I saw no temple therein, for the Lord God Almighty and the Lamb are the temple of it. And the city had no need of the sun, neither of the moon to shine in it, for the glory of God did lighten it, and the Lamb is the light thereof." What is the glory of Solomon's kingdom or temple, or of the world, if compared with the beauty of the new Jerusalem, which the most valuable things in nature, as gold and jewels, are used to set forth, but fall exceedingly short of what they signify!

Application

USE 1. It is matter of great lamentation that the Church at present is so far from edifying itself that it is doing quite the contrary. It is about to destroy and to pull itself down to the ground, if the God of wisdom, love, and peace does not hinder. The poet looked upon it as truly lamentable that the Roman state was engaged in a civil war where there could be no triumph after victory; that Pompey and Caesar, both brave, both Roman generals, should fight so eagerly, so bloodily one against the other. But surely 'tis one of the saddest sights in the world to see the members of the body of Christ at variance, and biting and devouring, and doing that to one another which the fiercest persecution was never able to effect. Alas, for woe, that the Church of Christ should be militant not only because of her fighting with enemies, but because of discord among her members!

The Church employs her own force to her own ruin. Pastors are set against pastors, saints against saints, sermons against sermons, nay, prayers against prayers, and Zion has become like a Babel of confusion!

Well may the prophet's words in Ezekiel 19:14 be here applied: "This is a lamentation, and shall be for a lamentation."

USE 2: of advice. Let the Church's edification be minded. Let all study and follow the things that make for peace, and things wherewith one may edify another (Romans 14:19). 'Tis not below the greatest of men to put their hands to this work of building the house of God; indeed, it should strenuously be set about by all: magistrates, ministers, and people.

1. The Church's edification is to be minded by magistrates. Their authority should be subservient to the authority of Him by whom they reign. Proverbs 8:15: "By me kings

reign, and princes decree justice." The laws of kingdoms and states should always promote and encourage the progress of the gospel. Truth and holiness do ever deserve the countenance of authority, but sin is worthy of a frown. Those princes who are most for the Church's welfare most consult their own. If "Righteousness exalteth a nation, and sin is the reproach and ruin of any people" (Proverbs 14:34), then the more the Church is edified, the more firmly both throne and kingdom are established. Hezekiah's zeal for religion was attended with a blessed prosperity. 2 Chronicles 31:21: "In every work that he began in the service of the house of God, and in the law, and in the commandments, to seek his God, he did it with all his heart, and he prospered."

2. The Church's edification is to be minded by ministers. 'Tis their office more peculiarly to be laborers together with God in His husbandry and building (1 Corinthians 3:9). They should pray, preach, and live so as to edify. Reputation and worldly advantage are poor things, but edification! Edification is most truly considerable, and should sound in their ears, should be upon their hearts, and should be endeavored with their utmost abilities. They must be blameless as the stewards of God, and faithfully dispense food to souls; they "must not be self-willed, not soon angry, not given to wine, no strikers, not given to filthy lucre; but lovers of hospitality, lovers of good men, sober, just, holy, temperate" (Titus 1:7–8). Then they are likely to build the house of God indeed!

3. The people also should endeavor the edification of the Church. They should, by a good example, provoke one another to love and good works. "No corrupt communication should proceed out of their mouths but that which is good to the use of edifying, and which may administer grace to the hearers" (Ephesians 4:29). They are to please one another for edification (Romans 15:2), and in all reproofs let love and a

desire to edify be apparent in the reprover.

I conclude with a few arguments to persuade all to edify the Church.

1. The Church of Christ is hugely out of repair. The breaches are great, and there is much rubbish to be removed. And where there is so much work to be done, the laborers should be the greater in number, and the more diligent.

2. While you are building His Church, the Lord Himself will be with you, and then no matter who the opposition is. Greater is He who is in you than he who is in the world. When Nehemiah was building Jerusalem, he was derided, he was opposed, but he was not discouraged, neither did the work cease; and the enemies were forced to an acknowledgment that God was with him.

3. Your labor shall not be in vain, either as to success or as to reward. Some good shall result if you desire it, and God takes notice how much more you would do, and will reward you accordingly. The Lord is too good a Master to suffer any of His faithful laborers and servants to lack encouragement. David had it in his heart to build Him a house; and God established the house of David (1 Chronicles 17:23). And his family was upheld till Christ, the Son of David, came. I am now done with the third proposition: the body of Christ should diligently endeavor to edify itself.

Chapter 4

Love Is for the Church's Edification

PROPOSITION 4. The more love abounds among the members of the Church, the more the whole body will be edified. Or, more briefly, love is exceedingly for the Church's edification. I might speak at great length in discoursing of love for Christ, and manifest how this will constrain all in whom it exists to seek the edification of His body, and to seek the welfare of those for whom He died. How can one who loves the Lord Jesus in sincerity choose but to love all saints, though of different persuasions, since, notwithstanding that difference, they are all so dear to Him that He gave His life as a ransom for them all? The blood of God was shed for every one of them that there might be a price paid sufficient for their redemption.

But the Apostle is to be understood in my original text as referring to Christian's love one for another. This is that charity for which the Scripture calls so loudly. John 13:34: "A new commandment I give unto you, that ye love one another; as I have loved you, that ye also love one another." The command is doubled, and called a new commandment because, though delivered long before, yet here 'tis delivered with a new example, that of Christ Himself ("as I have loved you"), and consequently with a new and strongly enforcing motive. The Apostle Peter gives this charge in 1 Peter 4:8: "Above all things have fervent charity among yourselves." Gifts, though excellent, may be abused and perversely employed to instill error and rend the Church of God. Knowledge, if it is alone, will not profit, but will puff up him who has it. But "charity edifieth" (1 Corinthians 8:1). Love is greatly beneficial; its acts are pure, peaceable, gentle, full of mercy and good fruits, and 'tis against the very nature of it to work ill to any.

In handling this proposition, I shall first discourse concerning the nature of love; second, uncover the properties which the Scripture attributes to it; third, demonstrate how it is for the Church's edification; fourth, show the vanity of those excuses that are made for the want of love; and, last, apply it all.

In the first place, I am to discourse concerning the nature of love. There are four types of love: carnal, natural, civil, and spiritual.

1. Carnal and impure. Thus Amnon loved his fair sister, Tamar, in 2 Samuel 13:1, and Samson fell in love with Delilah. But this impure affection cost both these their lives, and brought the one and the other to an untimely end. This may more properly be called lust than love; and in whatever heart 'tis harbored, how it defiles and hardens! If but a spark of lust is let alone, what a flame may quickly follow which may consume the estate, the reputation, the body and the soul! There may indeed be extenuating circumstances, but still 'tis threatened with the wrath of God. Not only for fornication, but for evil concupiscence the wrath of God comes upon the children of disobedience (Colossians 3:5–6). When lust is suffered to conceive and bring forth actual adultery, how do the adulterer and his strumpet show their hatred one for the other! The mischief they do themselves is inconceivable. And how do they defile the other's body, wound the other's conscience, and delight in that whereby they damn the other's soul!

2. Natural love, natural affection. To have this natural affection is a duty, for 'tis planted in the heart by the wise and gracious God as that which has a mighty tendency to the conservation of mankind. Therefore, the apostle describes being without natural affection as one of the crimes of those who were given up to "a reprobate mind to do those things which were not convenient" (Romans 1:28, 31). Natural affection we owe unto our relations, and if we refuse to pay this debt we shut our ears to the dictates of nature as well as the Word of Christ, and become worse than infidels, nay, worse than the beasts that perish. Parents must love their children, children their parents, husbands and wives must be full of affection toward one another. But grace should spiritualize this natural affection. Not only the persons of our relations must be loved, but their souls, and their eternal salvation most earnestly desired and endeavored. And if we cannot bear the thoughts of a parent's, husband's, wife's, or child's pain, poverty, slavery, or starving, the thoughts of their being eternally damned should be much more intolerable, and all means should be used to prevent it!

3. Civil. This is one of the great bonds of human societies whereby they are kept together, whereas hatred and discord first divide and then destroy them. The more our love for our country prevails, the more will our country flourish. In a kingdom, the whole should be concerned for every individual, every individual for the whole, and all the parts for one another. No member should hastily be concluded a gangrened one who is presently to be cut off, lest the whole community be endangered. Draco is not looked upon as one of the wisest legislators, who made almost every offense capital, and therefore is said to have written his laws in blood. A mild government, such as our English one is, best suits with Christianity, and is likeliest to attain the end of magistracy, the highest sovereign's glory, the king and kingdom's safety. Love should make all the subjects of a kingdom consider the relation they have to, and their concern for, one another. No plots and conspiracies should be allowed, but only designs and endeavors for one another's wealth and welfare—especially the truest wealth, and the welfare that is eternal.

I cannot here but bewail the lack of this civil love, and the variance of it that appears in my native country. New names of discrimination are invented which our forefathers knew not. Breaches grow wide as the sea, and who but the God of love and peace can heal them? A perverse spirit mingles itself among different parties; differences are kept up, and even increased with an unusual animosity.

And may not England, which at this day is in a flame of contention, be introduced thus speaking to her inhabitants? "O Englishmen, what causes us more harm than civil discord and fury among you? In me you have been born and bred. And considering the temperateness of the climate, the fruitfulness of the soil, and the variety of delights; where can you find a better land that might reasonably be wished to have been the land of your nativity? Be not, I beseech you, so unnatural as to fill and load me with sin, and to make me desolate, a land not inhabited. The corn I bear, the abundance of pleasant fruit I produce, the beasts I nourish for your food, the wholesome air you breath in—for all these, it would be an unworthy requital to turn me into an Akeldama, a field of blood. I have been a land of light to you, as well as fruitful. The sun of righteousness has shone as clearly and gloriously in me as in any nation under heaven. Oh, sin not, quarrel not away that which is my truest glory, that which is your greatest privilege. Study and mind the things which concern your peace. Make your peace with God by faith in His Son, and that faith accompanied with repentance and reformation; and be at peace among yourselves. And then you need not fear your foreign foes. And I should again become a land of renown, and be both feared and courted all Europe over."

4. A love which is spiritual. The grounds and attractions of this love are spiritual; and this is the kind of love of which our primary text speaks. Christian hearts should be filled with it. And the more this is expressed, the more the Church must be edified. The nature of this love I shall explain in these particulars.

(1) Love is a grace wrought by the God of all grace. 1 John 4:7: "Let us love one another; for love is of God, and everyone that loveth is born of God, and knoweth God." That Spirit which brings a man to the knowledge of God, and regenerates him and makes him a new creature, works in him this grace of love. Therefore we read that the fruit of the Spirit is love (Galatians 5:22). Though good nature is an excellent thing, and the dispositions of many incline them to be full of loving-kindness, yet this natural sweetness of temper greatly differs from Christian charity. The best nature is regardless of the soul; neither is it concerned for itself or others beyond the things of sense and of this present world. The Apostle thus describes a state of nature in which he sometimes was as well as others. Titus 3:3: "We ourselves were sometimes foolish, disobedient, deceived, serving divers lusts and pleasures, living in malice and envy, hateful and hating one another." So that true love to others is of a heavenly origin.

(2) Love is in obedience to the divine command. Christians love one another because their Lord and Savior has commanded them to do so. John 15:12: "This is My commandment, that ye love one another as I have loved you." Both law and gospel insist upon this. The sum of the second table of the law is this: "Thou shalt love thy neighbor as thyself." And by the gospel this law is established. Faith in Christ, therefore, and love are joined. 1 John 3:23: "And this is His

commandment, that we should believe on the name of His
Son Jesus Christ, and love one another as He gave us commandment." Obedience to the command sanctifies our love
for our neighbor, and renders it not only more profitable to
him, but acceptable to God Himself. When we love others
that God's will may be fulfilled and He may be pleased, and
because of the image of God and Christ which we see in
them, then we love truly. And this is the meaning of 1 John
5:2: "By this we know that we love the children of God, when
we love God, and keep His commandments," that is, when
love for God, and a care to keep His laws, induce us to love
His children, because He bids us and for His sake.

(3) Love implies a mortification of contrary passions.
The poet says, "Virtue is to fly from vice." So may I say, love is
to fly from anger, wrath, malice, bitterness, envy, and revenge,
which are sins of such a nature that they carry their punish-
ment in their bowels, and *make* a hell as well as *deserve* one.
The darkness of the night is chased away when the day returns and the sun rises; sickness is removed when health is restored. And in like manner those sinful and corrupt passions
which benight the soul, and are the diseases of it, are purged
out where this grace of love is indeed infused. The Apostle
plainly shows this in Ephesians 4:31 and 5:2. In the former
verse he says, "Let all bitterness, and wrath, and anger, and
clamor be put away, with all kind of malice." In the latter he
says, "Walk in love, as Christ also hath loved us, and gave Himself for us." Compare also Colossians 3:8 with verse 14 and you
may perceive that we must put off anger, wrath, and malice
when we "put on charity, which is the bond of perfectness."

(4) Love implies an inclination to union. The nature
of it is to unite and knit things together. Thus, by the love of
friendship, the soul of Jonathan was knit with the soul of
David (1 Samuel 18:1); and the hearts of Christians are knit

together by this excellent grace of love (Colossians 2:2). Union is of God, and is indeed the Church's strength. The bundle of rods in the fable, while they remained bound together, could not be broken, whereas every single one might be snapped asunder with ease. So far as the Church is divided, so far 'tis certainly and dangerously weakened.

There is an admirable union in the Godhead. Three distinct persons are in one incomprehensibly glorious nature. There is a wonderful union also in Christ Himself: two distinct natures in one person and mediator. And these two natures differ infinitely more than earth and heaven, than the sun and a molehill, and yet behold them inseparably united. The Church's union is mystical: there are many members, but love makes them one body; for it makes them of one heart and of one soul. Love alters the contentious and cruel nature, and inclines to union and peace. So that, to use the prophet's phrase, "The wolf dwells peaceably with the lamb, and the leopard lies down with the kid, and the calf and the young lion and the fatling together; and a little child may lead them. The cow and the bear feed, their young ones lie down together, and the lion eats straw like the ox. The sucking child plays on the hole of the asp, and the weaned child puts his hand on the adder's den." So far as love prevails, there is no hurting or destroying one another in all God's holy mountain (Isaiah 11:6–9). Christ prayed for this union, as that which would be for the Church's benefit and the world's conviction that He came forth from God. John 17:21: "That they all may be one, as Thou, Father, art in Me, and I in Thee; that they also may be one in Us, that the world may believe that Thou hast sent Me." How needful is love to unite Christians and make them one, since divisions strike at Christ Himself and harden the world in its infidelity!

(5) Love enlarges the heart and frees it from the bonds

of selfishness, and makes us desire others' welfare as well as
our own. Love for our neighbor breathes forth in fervent
wishes that it may be well with him, both in time and to eternity. We are in every respect to consider our brethren; and
true love will make us long that in every way they may be benefited; that they may not want any needful secular comfort
and encouragement; especially that they may be blessed with
all spiritual blessings, and, above all, that they may attain eternal happiness and salvation. The Apostle's love vents itself in
a prayer for the Corinthians' temporal prosperity and increase. 2 Corinthians 9:10: "Now may He that ministereth
seed to the sower both minister bread for your food and
multiply your seed sown, and increase the fruits of your
righteousness." So John, writing to his beloved Gaius, wishes
him health and prosperity in 3 John 2: "Beloved, I wish above
all things that thou mayst prosper and be in health, even as
thy soul prospereth." But the Apostle's wishes that souls might
be sanctified and saved were most vehemently and
pathetically expressed in Romans 10:1: "Brethren, my heart's
desire and prayer to God for Israel is that they might be
saved." Philippians 1:8: "God is my record how greatly I long
after you all in the bowels of Jesus Christ." Galatians 4:19: "My
little children of whom I travail in birth again until Christ be
formed in you." Behold, how the Apostle loved souls! I don't
wonder that he offers his love as a blessing to the church in
1 Corinthians 16:24: "My love be with you all in Christ Jesus.
Amen."

(6) Love is the fulfilling of the law, the doing of which
is so much for our neighbor's benefit. Romans 13:8: "He that
loveth another, hath fulfilled the law." As love for God includes the whole first table of the law, so love for our neighbor includes the second: with reason 'tis called the fulfilling
of the law, for it causes an affectionate and obedient respect

unto every commandment of the second table. And there is not one of these precepts but 'tis hugely for the good of mankind.

Love has a regard to the honor and authority of others. That honor which is due to natural parents, love is ready to yield. They who were instrumental in giving us our very being, and who nourished us with such tenderness and care when we were not able to shift for ourselves, may rightly challenge obedience from us. Upon a supposition that parents are fallen into decay, that piety that children show them in relieving them is called requiting them (1 Timothy 5:4), so that children's disobedience, as 'tis unnatural, so it has a great deal of ingratitude in it.

Love ascends higher than our natural parents, and reaches the very thrones where kings and princes are placed. Kings are *patriae patres,* fathers of their country. All the inhabitants of a kingdom are the children of the king, and as they have a common father their very hearts should love and reverence him. It was not a court compliment or a strain of rhetoric, but an expression of religious loyalty when the prophet called the anointed of the Lord the breath of the people's nostrils (Lamentations 4:20), and signifies how dear his life should be unto them all. Love will cause tribute and custom to be willingly paid, fear and honor to be rendered (Romans 13:7).

Christian princes, according as it was prophetically promised (Isaiah 49:23), are the Church's nursing fathers. The Church of Christ in this world has not arrived at such maturity that it stands in no need of nursing; the magistrate's care is needful, and his authority is a good fence unto the Christian faith. And if the doctrine of the gospel has a legal establishment, how should this endear the supreme Magistrate unto all inferiors! Where Christian love reigns in the hearts of subjects, there Christian kings will reign with greater security. Love and rightly informed conscience, wherever found, will do more than rods and axes (though these are also necessary) to support and defend the civil government.

Love has a regard to the lives of others. The guilt of blood is great; the cry of blood is loud. Murder! how does it wound the murderer's conscience, and defile the very land which receives the blood of him who is murdered! Love utterly abhors cruelty and slaughter. It considers the meekness and gentleness of Christ. When James and John would, by miraculous fire, have consumed a Samaritan village that would not receive their Lord, He rebuked them, and said, "Ye know not what manner of spirit ye are of; for the Son of Man is not come to destroy men's lives but to save them" (Luke 9:55–56). Love is so far from thirsting after blood that it will not allow malice in the heart; nay, rash and causeless anger it dislikes, for that will make a man in danger of the judgment (Matthew 5:22). Were but love everywhere revived, it would put an end to the iron age and cause the golden age to return. Swords would be beaten into plowshares, spears into pruning hooks, and nations would not learn war any more.

Love will not violate others' chastity. Lust is strongly inclined to such a violation, but the grace of love is of a holy and clean nature, and abhors all obscenity. It is so far from consenting to defile another's body that it will not allow the heart, even by a filthy thought or desire, to be defiled. For our Lord says, "Whosoever looketh on a woman to lust after her hath committed adultery with her already in his heart" (Matthew 5:28). Love looks upon the bodies of Christians as members of Christ, as temples of the Spirit. Now the members of Christ are not to be polluted; the temples of the Spirit are not to be profaned. How little of true love is there in this lustful age, in this adulterous generation! An affection that is indeed Christian is rarely to be found, but a reprobate and brutish concupiscence is very rife both in city and country, though hereby both are ripening apace for vengeance. Jeremiah 5:7–9: " 'They assembled themselves by troops in the harlots' houses. They were as fed horses in the morning; everyone neighed after his neighbor's wife. Shall I not visit for these things,' saith the Lord, 'and shall not My soul be avenged on such a nation as this?' "

Love will not steal away the substance of another. It abhors to be injurious to any; it is for following that which is altogether just. It is ready to distribute, willing to share with the poor, according to that charge in 1 Timothy 6:18; and the poorer any are, love is so much the more generous. Love is liberal: "For he that soweth sparingly shall reap sparingly, and he which soweth bountifully shall reap bountifully" (2 Corinthians 9:6). But though it will give away pounds to those who are needy, it dares not unjustly take away a penny or a farthing from another, though never so wealthy. Solomon tells us that a "false balance is not good, and unjust weights are an abomination to the Lord" (Proverbs 20:23); and they are also an abomination to love. No duty is more clearly discovered by the light of nature than to do justly; and what does God in His written Word more expressly require? The unrighteous are plainly threatened with the loss of the kingdom of heaven; and what poor and petty things are their unjust gains compared with such a kingdom! Wronging another, though it is in so sly a manner that human eyes observe it not, cannot be punished by human laws; yet it will be overtaken with divine vengeance. 1 Thessalonians 4:6: "That no man go beyond and defraud his brother in any matter, because the Lord is the avenger of all such, as we also have forewarned you and testified." Love for our neighbor implies a love of justice, which is to give our neighbor his due.

Love can as soon cease to be love as it can begin to be injurious. Nay, if a man has heretofore been guilty of injustice, it will incline and constrain him to make restitution, for "The wicked must restore the pledge, and give again what he hath robbed, and walk in the statutes of life; then he shall live, he shall not die" (Ezekiel 33:15).

Love is very tender of others' names and reputations. It detests all manner of lying as that which is an abomination to God (Proverbs 6:17), and exposes the liar himself to the burning lake (Revelation 21:8). But a slanderous or malicious lie that wounds the name and murders the reputation of another, it hates exceedingly; for this is an abomination most abominable, and more against the very letter of the law: "Thou shalt not bear false witness against thy neighbor." The name of a man ought to be very dear to him, especially if he is a Christian, because God, Christ, and the gospel are concerned in it. A Christian cannot have aspersions cast on him without some aspersion on Christianity itself. Love is very wary, and that with great reason, and will not cast into the precious ointment a dead fly to make it send forth an evil savor. Love hinders the tongue from evil speaking, and makes it subject to the law of kindness. Love is so far from raising a false report of another that it dares not take it up, much less spread it all abroad. This is part of the character of the citizen of Zion who shall dwell with God both here and forever: "He speaketh the truth in his heart; he backbiteth not with his tongue, nor doeth evil to his neighbor, nor taketh up a reproach against his neighbor" (Psalm 15:2–3).

Light may as well become darkness, as love be guilty of lying and malicious defamations. Professors' ears are ready to tingle when they hear the sound of hellish oaths and horrid execrations, wretched men making bold with the life of God and the blood and wounds of Christ, and hardly a sentence being pronounced without an imprecation that God may damn them. But these professors would do well to consider that the same mouth of truth which has forbidden and threatened cursing and swearing has forbidden and threatened lying and slandering; and if we observe how much injury may be done by a slanderous tongue, we shall not wonder that the throats of such slanderers are compared to open sepulchers, and their tongues to whetted swords and sharpened arrows, and the poison of asps is said to be under them.

Love is contented with its own, and hinders us from coveting what belongs to another. Sinful lust and desire after that which is our neighbor's precipitate those acts whereby he is injured. Thus Ahab's inordinate desire after Naboth's vineyard made him a murderer of Naboth (and that with many aggravations) that he might enjoy it. Love breeds contentment, and instead of coveting what is another's it wishes him both a quiet possession and a holy improvement. And love, expelling these inordinate lusts, plucks up the very root of bitterness from whence commonly grow all those injuries that the sons of men do one to another. Thus love is eagle-eyed to observe whatever God in His law has commanded for our neighbor's good; and since the wise and gracious Lawgiver has manifested His care of our neighbor in fencing his life and all that is dear to him with so many commandments, love rationally infers that it ought to be our care not to break this fence, but to keep all these commandments without exception.

Love breeds sympathy when our fellow Christians are in misery. It makes us fear lest harm befall the Church of God; and when the Church is actually under affliction it causes us in that affliction to be afflicted. Love is the great law of Christ, and Christian sympathy is a fulfilling of it. Galatians 6:2: "Bear ye one another's burdens, and so fulfill the law of Christ." The captive Jews' harps were out of tune, and their hearts had lit-

tle tendency to mirth and music; nay, "By the rivers of
Babylon they wept when they remembered Zion" (Psalm
137:1). Love easily melts the heart of a saint into sorrow when
other saints are in sadness and calamity; nay, 'tis ready to put
on compassion when it sees any in misery. This sympathy of
love is a real thing, and shows itself in a forwardness to relieve
and help. Love enlarges the heart in prayer for the distressed
Church of Christ and all His members. It makes us, as we observe the Church's languors, ready to faint and die away ourselves. Love draws forth our compassion towards the divided
and distressed land of our nativity. And in some it arises to so
high a degree that they are ready (such are their holy ago-
nies) to wish their names blotted out of the Book of Life, and
themselves accursed from Christ, rather than England should
become desolate, rather than God should depart and the glorious gospel of our Lord Jesus Christ be removed!

Love makes us delight in the communion of the saints. Sin has
brought a great deformity and unloveliness upon mankind.
The Scripture speaks thus of men, considered in their natural
state: "They are all gone aside, they are all together become
filthy; there is none that doeth good, no, not one" (Psalm
14:3). But the grace of God has made a difference between
the saints and other men, in that they have "put off the old
man which is corrupt according to deceitful lusts, and put on
the new man which after God is created in righteousness and
true holiness" (Ephesians 4:22, 24). Now this holiness makes
them truly amiable. Love makes us pity the world that lies in
wickedness, but delight in those who by regeneration are
called out of the world and made new creatures. David,
though a king, looked upon saints as the excellent ones, and
his delight was all in them as the most eligible and suitable
society (Psalm 16:3). Love is exceedingly pleased with the
holy, unblamable, and exemplary lives of others. It finds a

melody and sweetness in their gracious and edifying dis-
courses, when their hearts are warm and their graces are in
vigorous exercise. The delight is greatest when saints are most
like themselves, revealing the most of real sanctity and the
least of sinful infirmity. Love is for communion with all saints,
though of different persuasions. It is a sign that a man is fond
of his own opinion if he likes saints of his own judgment only,
and that his complacency is not so truly in the image of God
wherever it shines. 'Tis want of light that makes saints of different sentiments in religion, and 'tis want of love that makes
them so shy, to look so strangely, to speak so strangely, and to
act so strangely one towards another.

Love causes a joy in the good of others. In the natural body, "if
one member be honored, all the members rejoice with it"
(1 Corinthians 12:26). Christians in like manner are "to rejoice with them that do rejoice" (Romans 12:15). It was an excellent spirit in John the Baptist, and it argued the truth of his
love for the Messiah, of whom he was the forerunner, that he
rejoiced to see Christ increase, though he himself decreased
(John 3:29–30). The Apostle was persuaded of the
Corinthians' affection for him when he said, "I have confidence in you all, that my joy is the joy of you all" (2 Corinthians 2:3). The more love abounds, the more the joy of one
Christian will be the joy of every one. Love rejoices to see the
Spirit of God poured out in the most plentiful manner, to see
useful and excellent gifts distributed to others. It is really glad
of their highest attainments, their enlargements, their comforts, their honor and esteem following upon all this. We are
all members one of another; and why should we not rejoice in
one another's honor since we are really honored one in
another, and the honor of all redounds at length to our Lord
Jesus Christ, who is the Head of all?

Love covers a multitude of sins and infirmities (1 Peter 4:8). Not that there is any merit in this grace of charity to deserve the pardon of sin in ourselves; but instead of spreading the faults of others it spreads a veil over them. Love makes us tender-hearted and kind, ready to forgive others, as we ourselves, for Christ's sake, have been forgiven. And indeed the offenses and injuries done to us by others are but like the debt of a few pence compared with our offenses against God, which amount to many millions of talents. The Apostle Peter asked Christ, "Lord, how often shall my brother sin against me, and I forgive him? Till seven times? Jesus saith unto him, 'I say unto thee, not till seven times, but until seventy times seven' " (Matthew 18:21–22). Some think that there is allusion to the custom of the Jews to show favor every seventh year, and especially in the year of Jubilee. As there is a greater measure of light in the Christian church than there was in the Jewish, so ought there to be a greater measure of love. We must not only forgive seven times, or seven times seven, but seventy times seven; a certain number for an uncertain, intimating we must pardon our trespassing brother without any stint or limitation. Our Lord calls the time of the gospel "the acceptable year" (Luke 4:19). Christians should abhor all manner of revenge, and be as charitably inclined to pass by their brethren's faults as if their life were a perpetual Jubilee.

Where is the love of those who not only harbor in their hearts a grudge against their brethren, but whose mouths are like trumpets to sound forth their failings? Nay, they tarry not to examine whether they are truly failings or not, but boldly and blindly conclude them to be such, and proclaim and exclaim against them. Nay, their eager tongues tarry not for a verified information; but whether reports to the disparagement of others be true or false, they spread them like wildfire. What's become of love all the while? Love hides a multitude of sins, but these persons won't conceal one. Love covers real crimes, but these forbear not spreading false reports. The tongue is called by Drexelius the Phaethon of the world that sets it a flame. If, as the apostle says, an unruly tongue defiles the whole body, and he who seems religious and bridles not his tongue does but deceive his own heart, and his religion is in vain (James 1:26), then let a multitude of professors at this day tremble and be astonished, and cry out, "who among us shall be saved?"

Love is projecting and designing the good of others. Thus the Apostle abased himself that others might be exalted, and sought not his own profit, but the profit of many, that they might be saved (1 Corinthians 10:33). Love works no ill to one's neighbor, but is very fruitful in contriving, and operative in promoting, his neighbor's welfare. Love is not in "word and in tongue only, but in deed and in truth" (1 John 3:18). It will not only say, "Depart in peace, be ye warmed and filled" (James 2:16), but 'tis ready to clothe the naked and to feed the hungry. Nay, it devises liberal and charitable things, and considers the wants of souls as well as bodies cordially, according to its capacity, endeavoring that both may be supplied. The Apostle's love for the Corinthians was very active, notwithstanding a woeful failing on their side. 2 Corinthians 12:14–15: "I seek not yours, but you; and I will very gladly spend and be spent for you [in the Greek it is "for your souls"], though the more abundantly I love you, the less I be loved." Thus have I explained the nature of love.

Chapter 5

The Properties of Love

In the second place I am to speak of the properties which the Scripture attributes to love, and requires should be in it.

1. Love must proceed from a pure heart (1 Timothy 1:5). A heart must of necessity be made a new one before this grace of love can dwell there. If Satan cannot make us hate our brother, he will endeavor to defile our love. There is need of greater care that our love be not defiled by selfishness, or by lust and filthiness. Our affections should be pure and clean, as angels may be conceived to love one another. All impure motions must be detested utterly; and our hearts, being first circumcised to love a God of holiness, must love saints for their holiness' sake. Our love should always have a holy aim, and never degenerate so as to design the polluting of others, or ourselves with them.

2. Love must be joined with a good conscience (1 Timothy 1:5). A Christian should not be conscious within himself of any sinful or ulterior motives in his love for others. He must not hold persons in admiration because it is to his advantage, nor allow for any hypocrisy, which conscience cannot choose if it is tender, but condemn. Therefore, says the apostle, "Let love be without dissimulation" (Romans 12:9). Conscience observes whether our inward affection is consistent with our speeches, our shows, and our pretenses, and should be able to bear witness to our integrity. Our love for our neighbors should be for Christ's sake, and should make us pursue the ends for which Christ died on their account.

3. Love must flow from faith unfeigned. In 1 Timothy 1:5 we read: "Now the end of the commandment is charity out of a pure heart, and of a good conscience, and of faith unfeigned." There must be a firm belief in God's goodwill toward men, of Christ's love for His Church so as to give Himself for its redemption and salvation, and that He much insists upon this command, that Christians should love one another. And when love is the product of this belief, then 'tis right, then 'tis acceptable. The Apostle gave thanks without ceasing on behalf of the Ephesians when he heard of their faith in the Lord Jesus, and their love for all the saints (Ephesians 1:15–16). How can he refuse to love any one saint who unfeignedly believes that Christ died for all—especially if withal he is upon good grounds persuaded that Christ loved him, and gave Himself for him.

4. Love must be fervent. 1 Peter 1:22: "Seeing ye have purified your souls in obeying the truth through the Spirit, unto unfeigned love of the brethren, see that ye love one another with a pure heart fervently." It is ill with the body if the natural heat abates; it argues a dangerous decay in the new creature if love waxes cold. If Christians' love one towards another languishes, proportionably there will be also a languishing of their love for Christ Himself, and this is very perilous. When there was not a fervency, but lukewarmness in Laodicea, Christ threatened to spew her out of His mouth (Revelation 3:16). When Ephesus had left her first love, He said, "I will come unto thee quickly, and remove thy candlestick out of this place, except thou repent" (Revelation 2:5). The great love of God in Christ, His frequent injunctions that love may continue, the excellency, sweetness, usefulness, and even absolute necessity of love for the Church's conservation—all this should be as perpetual fuel to maintain this holy fire.

5. Christians' love must be brotherly. Christ said to His

disciples, "All ye are brethren" (Matthew 23:8). The whole
body of believers is called "the brotherhood" in 1 Peter 2:17.
Christians are all children of the same heavenly Father who,
by one Spirit, according to His abundant mercy, has begotten
them again to a lively hope. All of them have Christ as their elder Brother, and are born again of the same seed which is incorruptible. How reasonable, then, are those injunctions:
"Love as brethren" (1 Peter 3:8), and "let brotherly love continue" (Hebrews 13:1). Alas, for woe! that the sinful defects
and passions of brethren are to be found among professors,
but not the affection! Multitudes at this day resemble the
brother spoken of by Solomon in Proverbs 18:19: "A brother
offended is harder to be won than a strong city, and their
contentions are like the bars of a castle."

6. Love should be extended so as to become universal; and
the more extensive it is, the more it makes a man resemble
God Himself.

(1) Love is to be extended to the whole church, to all
saints. When love is limited to a party, 'tis imprisoned, as it
were, which ought to enjoy the greatest liberty. 'Tis common
and needful to distinguish between conversion to a party and
conversion to God. There is a distinction likewise to be made
between love for a party and love for the Church of God. 'Tis
but too apparent that men place too much in being of such a
party and persuasion, and therefore all receding, though
done with a clear conscience, and for the Church's peace, is
nicknamed "apostasy." And though a man walks as closely
with God, lives as well as ever, loves more saints, and loves the
saints more than ever, yet because he is not rigidly of such a
way he is censured, belied, reproached and shunned, as if he
were a heathen man or publican. Oh, love! Why do you sleep?
Awake, awake! Wherever you are planted, revive and flourish
and bring forth the fruits of kindness, peaceableness, tender-

ness and moderation! All true saints of all persuasions are beloved of God and purchased with His blood, and nothing shall be able to separate them from the love of God which is in Christ Jesus their Lord (Romans 8:39). Disaffections, therefore, and distances one from another are very unseemly, very sinful. Though God loves all His children freely, yet they are all worthy of one another's love, and this love is the just debt which they owe one to another. If saints are as saints, all saints will be loved. And if we love not all, 'tis but all too plain that we love none at all truly.

(2) Love is to be extended to the Jews, since they are beloved for their Father's sake (Romans 11:28). Christians should love them, and express that love by prayer that they may not still abide in their unbelief, but look unto Jesus whom they have pierced and obtain mercy.

(3) Love is to reach unto the uncalled Gentiles. The world's blindness and wickedness should move our compassion; and since the mercy of our God is so inconceivably large we should desire that more may partake of it. And since Christ is a propitiation sufficient for the sins of the whole world (1 John 2:2), we should pity the millions of souls who never heard of Him, and beg that the sound of the gospel may come to their ears, and that through this Jesus they may be reconciled and saved.

(4) Love is to be extended even to enemies and persecutors. Christians must not render evil for evil, reproach for reproach, cursing for cursing; but if they are reviled, they are to bless; if they are defamed, they are to entreat; and they must endeavor the world's benefit, though they are made the filth of the world and the off-scouring of all things (1 Corinthians 4:12–13). A saint's patience should always be greater than the passion of a persecutor, a saint's love greater than a persecutor's hatred. 'Tis an excellent spirit, and the right spirit of

Christian charity, to be meek and kind to those who are most bitter against us; to speak the best of those who speak the worst of us; to pray that our most spiteful enemies may be forgiven, and that the injuries which are done us, being pardoned, may not do an eternal harm unto the injurers.

7. Love should never fail, but should more and more increase. It must be a constant fire never to be extinguished; nay, it should become stronger and purer continually. Philippians 1:9: "And this I pray, that your love may abound yet more and more in knowledge and in all judgment." The true reasons of love must be better and better understood, and the expressions of love must be still with more and more judgment and discretion that the end aimed at may be attained. After the apostle had acknowledged that the Thessalonians were taught of God to love one another, yet he added, "We beseech you, brethren, that you increase more and more" (1 Thessalonians 4:9–10). And if where love did so much abound there was reason to urge an increase, oh, how much need is there in such an angry and contentious age as this to blow up this fire which is so near to going out! I am now done with the properties of love.

Chapter 6

How Love Is for the Church's Edification

In the third place I am to demonstrate how love is for the Church's edification. 'Tis for the edification of those whom a Christian loves. A Christian edifies both himself and others by love. First, I shall demonstrate that he edifies himself.

1. The more he loves, there is the greater light in him. The understanding is darkened by those sins which are contrary to love, such as prejudice, passion, envy, or hatred, so that what is truth is not easily discerned, and what is duty is not readily apprehended in many cases. The aforementioned evil affections bias the judgment wrongly. Though the eye is good, and the object not far off, yet the eye cannot so plainly see the object if there is a mist between them. Anger and malice raise such a mist before the eye of the judgment that 'tis very prone to be mistaken; but this mist is scattered by love, so that a Christian sees his way plain and is less subject to stumble. 1 John 2:9–11: "He that saith he is in the light, and hateth his brother, is in darkness even until now. He that loveth his brother abideth in the light, and there is no occasion of stumbling in him; but he that hateth his brother is in darkness, and walketh in darkness, and knoweth not whither he goeth, because that darkness hath blinded his eyes."

2. The more a Christian loves, there is the more of God's image in him; he is the more transformed into the divine nature. 1 John 4:7–8: "God is love, and everyone that loveth is born of God, and knoweth God." In Scripture God is said to delight in mercy, to rest in His love, to be good to all, to be

kind to the unthankful and evil. How does love edify a child
of God, making him resemble his heavenly Father in these
excellent perfections; and how unlike Satan does love make
us! Have we knowledge? How great an understanding has the
evil one! Have we faith? The devils also believe and tremble;
but if we have love, Satan has nothing of this in him. He hates
and tortures his own self; he hates God's children, and all his
own children. He would destroy the former; and he will, unless they cease to be his children, destroy the latter.

3. The more a Christian loves, the more firm is his evidence that he is indeed a Christian. The Apostle tells us that
the fruit of the Spirit is love, joy, and peace. The more love,
the more peace and joy (Galatians 5:22). We read in
Philippians 2:1 of "consolation in Christ and comfort in love."
Love builds us up in solid comfort; for we have the mark of
Christ's sheep upon us if we love the whole flock. That religion has not truth that has not love in it. Pretenses to light
and purity, without love, are all vain. But he who is full of love
in this world shall not be sent to hell in the other world,
where there is no love at all. 1 John 3:14: "We know that we
have passed from death to life, because we love the brethren."

Second, I shall demonstrate that Christians edify not only
themselves but others by their love, and that it is exceedingly
for the Church's edification.

1. Love makes us concerned for the whole Church of
Christ, and enlarged in our supplications and intercessions
for it. This public spirit, which is the effect of universal love, is
very pleasing unto God, and mightily prevails with Him. God
encourages us to an importunity for Zion. He does not say, as
He did to Moses, "Let Me alone that I may destroy," but "give
Me no rest" until I save. Isaiah 62:6–7: "I have set watchmen
upon thy walls, O Jerusalem, which shall never hold their

peace day nor night. Ye that make mention of the Lord, keep
not silence, and give Him no rest till He establish and make
Jerusalem a praise in the earth." Love takes this encouragement, and makes the Christian thus to resolve: "For Zion's
sake I will not hold My peace, and for Jerusalem's sake I will
not rest, until the righteousness thereof goes forth as brightness, and the salvation thereof as a lamp that burneth" (Isaiah
62:1). The Church's reformation and righteousness are to be
prayed for as well as its deliverance and salvation. The apostle
tells us that if we would pray effectively, we must lift up holy
hands without wrath and doubting (1 Timothy 2:8). Wrath
defiles him who prays, and fills the censer with strange fire,
mixing a sinful fervency and heat with prayer, and so hinders
its prevailing and acceptance. But love empties the heart of
wrath, and fills it with a holy furor. And how much does the
effectual, fervent prayer of a righteous man prevail (James
5:16). Moses was full of love for Israel and for the God of
Israel; he was zealous for God's honor, and desirous of Israel's
welfare. He stood in the gap, and by prayer turned away that
wrath that was breaking in and ready to destroy all the people.
Psalm 106:23: "Therefore He said that He would destroy
them, had not Moses His chosen stood in the breach before
Him, to turn away His wrath lest He should destroy them."

2. Love strongly inclines us unto peaceableness, and what
is for the Church's peace is for her edification. Romans 14:19:
"Let us follow after the things that make for peace, and things
wherewith one may edify another." I grant that when we are
pursuing peace we must have a special regard for truth and
holiness. Zechariah 8:19: "Love the truth and peace,"
Hebrews 12:14: "Follow after peace with all men, and holiness." But the Scripture must determine what is truth, and we
must distinguish between the great truths of the gospel and
those that are less important. It was a truth, which the Apostle

was persuaded of by the Lord Jesus Christ, that there was no meat unclean of itself; and yet those who were otherwise persuaded he looked upon as tolerable, and not to be despised. Nay, he expressly forbids those of different sentiments in this matter to judge one another (Romans 14). The Scripture likewise must inform us wherein purity and holiness lies; for a mistake here may quickly draw forth such a furious zeal as may set the Church in a flame. Some view purity and all religion as being established by the liturgy, as if the compilers of it had been divinely inspired, and all other prayer were but mere enthusiasm and contemptible babbling. On the other hand, some place purity and all religion in declaiming against the liturgy, calling it the mark of the beast and the very voice of the whore of Babylon. But neither the one nor the other views purity and religion rightly.

The Scripture nowhere commands that we should only pray by form; neither does it forbid a form to be used. But it requires that our very hearts and souls should be in our prayers, and faith and holy desires and other graces exercised in our duties—here lies the purity of them. Love, therefore, refuses to be quarrelsome about smaller matters; for it knows that peaceableness cements the Church and closes her breaches. And it justly fears lest while men are so contentious about ceremonies the substance of religion is lost in the quarrel.

3. Love makes Christians condescend and yield one to another, that hereby edification may be promoted. To be magisterial and self-willed is not to be the servants of Christ who are employed in building His Church. We are not to be dictators, but are alike to hearken to the voice and command of Christ our Lord, and to be mild and gentle one towards another. The Apostle Peter charges the younger to submit themselves to the elder, but withal adds, "Yea, all of you be subject one to

another" (1 Peter 5:5), and hereby intimates that to be lordly and imposing is contrary to the spirit of Christianity. It was love that made the Apostle Paul a servant to all that he might gain the more (1 Corinthians 9:19). To the Jews he became as a Jew that he might gain the Jews; to the weak he became as weak that he might gain the weak. He did not hereby manifest a carnal compliance through fear, but a condescension of love. He was not to be charged with levity or apostasy; he was not to be censured as a turncoat, as a hypocrite, as a mongrel minister; nor was he called dough-baked, a cake not turned. No, no, the Apostle loved the gospel, and had a mind to spread it. He loved souls and was desirous to save them, and understood how far he might yield in indifferent things for the Church's peace and edification.

Love makes us patient and self-denying; it hinders us from pursuing petty designs or private revenges. Pleasing God and profiting His Church swallow up such things as these. Love will hinder us from minding high things, and move us to condescend to men of low estate (Romans 12:16). Indeed, it makes us apply ourselves to all the best and most probable ways to secure their benefit. We shall endeavor to help the weak; we shall pity the fallen; we shall labor to reduce the straying; we shall encourage the diligent and honor the stronger saints—and all this is hugely for edification.

4. Love makes Christians highly esteem the pastors and builders of the Church for their work's sake; and hereby edification is promoted. The ministry of the gospel is a special gift which Christ bestowed upon His Church for her inconceivable advantage. Ephesians 4:8, 11–13: "Wherefore He saith, when He ascended up on high He led captivity captive and gave gifts unto men. And He gave some apostles, and some prophets, and some evangelists, and some pastors and teachers, for the perfecting of the saints, for the work of the

ministry, for the edifying of the body of Christ; till we all come
in the unity of the faith and of the knowledge of the Son of
God, unto a perfect man." And since the ministry is such a gift
and token of the royal bounty of Christ who is ascended far
above all heavens, certainly the flock of Christ is to love and
encourage its pastors. And the more they do this, the more
likely it is that the end of the ministry's institution should be
attained, namely the edifying and perfecting of the Church of
Christ. The Apostle, though he might have commanded, yet
uses entreaties for ministers' sake (1 Thessalonians 5:12–13).
He had bid them just before (verse 11) to "edify one another," but knowing the work of edification would go on but
lamely without a gospel ministry, he therefore adds: "And we
beseech you, brethren, to know them which labor among you,
and are over you in the Lord, and admonish you, and to esteem them very highly in love for their work's sake, and be at
peace among yourselves."

5. Love will constrain the pastors and builders of the
Church to mind their work to purpose. A minister who is full
of love for Christ and souls cannot be a loiterer. If indeed he
desires preferment, and if to fill his bags with wealth is his
great aim, then he will begrudge souls his pains. He will not
be concerned, though hell fills never so fast, and though he is
going quickly there himself. But if holy love for the Church of
Christ rules in his heart, it will constrain him to be a laborer,
and to do his work diligently. He will watch and pray; he will
search and study, and, above all books, the Bible. He will take
heed to himself, and to all his flock, that he may save himself
and those who hear him. Nay, love will make a minister labor,
and suffer also for the Church's edification. Abundant love
for the Corinthians made the apostle say, "I will very gladly
spend and be spent for you" (2 Corinthians 12:15). And 'tis
very plain that he did not think much of suffering. Philippians

2:17: "Yea, and if I be offered upon the sacrifice and service of your faith, I joy and rejoice with you all." These reasons plainly demonstrate how much love tends to edify.

But a great many reasons more I find all together, even a whole cluster of them (1 Corinthians 13:4–7), which I shall enlarge upon because they are both a trial of our love and a most evident demonstration that love is for edification. The Apostle's words are very searching, very piercing. He reads a kind of anatomy lecture upon this grace of love and charity, and lays the inside of it open to the view of others. He seems to speak a strange word: "Though I bestow all my goods to feed the poor, and have not charity, it profiteth me nothing" (verse 3). What is charity and love, some may say, if feeding the poor is not? These outward acts a Pharisee may do merely out of ostentation (Matthew 6). A papist may do as much, ignorantly hoping hereby to satisfy for his sins and merit heaven. I grant that love without these outward acts of mercy is vain and useless. Love in deed is love in truth (1 John 3:18). But though love produces such deeds, many outward acts of mercy may be performed where love is not present. The apostle, in a great many particulars, reveals true love and charity, and I shall make it evident how in every particular 'tis much for edification.

(1) Love suffers long and is kind. God is long-suffering, and so is love. It enables us to rule our own spirits, which argues true greatness and strength of soul. Proverbs 16:32: "He that is slow to anger is better than the mighty, and he that ruleth his spirit than he that taketh a city." Love is so far from avenging injuries already done that it will bear new ones. And that's the meaning of our Lord's injunction in Matthew 5:39: "I say unto you that ye resist not evil, but whosoever shall smite thee on the right cheek, turn to him the other also." Nay, love, though it suffers long, is kind notwithstanding. 'Tis

much to put up with an injury, but much more to be kind to the injurer. If this love were in churches, how would it unite them! And the more they are united, the more they are strengthened. Provocations to wrath would be turned into provocations to love, evil would be overcome by goodness; and the world hereby is likely to be convinced and converted. The proto-martyr Stephen was kind to those who stoned him. How he prayed that their sin might not be laid to their charge, but that their souls might be saved, though they thirsted after his blood and took away his life from him! This prayer was heard, and Saul, at length, was converted, and proved a master builder of the Church of God.

(2) Love envies not. It is not grieved and troubled at another's excellency; neither does it begrudge the comfort or prosperity of another. How much of hell is there in the temper of an envious man! The happiness of another is his misery, the good of another is his affliction. He looks upon the virtue of another with an evil eye, and is as sorry at the praise of another as if that praise were taken away from himself. Envy makes him a hater of his neighbor, and his own tormentor. Love flies from envy as extremely diabolical; for the root of it is pride, and ill will is its concomitant. What sad work has envy made in churches (not to speak of the mischief it has done all the world over), when Christians have been desirous of vain-glory, provoking one another, envying one another, which the apostle so much warns against in Galatians 5. When pastors have been envious of one another's parts, gifts, preferments, success and estimation, the poor Church has suffered, and its edification has gone on like Paul's work: very slowly. Envy makes the builders fall out, weaken one another's hands, and hinder one another in the work of God. Where envying and strife are, is there edification? By no means, but there is confusion and every evil work (James 3:16). Love, in-

stead of being troubled at the grace, usefulness, or esteem of another, rejoices therein; and the more there are who honor God, adorn the gospel, and benefit the Church, the more it rejoices.

(3) Love vaunteth not itself, neither is it puffed up. The word which the Holy Ghost uses for "vaunting" is *perpepeuetai*, a Greek word of Latin derivation, coming from *perperam*, which signifies "amiss." An ancient Greek Father, Basil, propounds the question, "What is *"perperpeuetai?"* and returns this answer: "Love is against doing things for show and ostentation, and excludes vain-glorious boasting." "Puffing up" relates to the heart, "vaunting" to the words and actions. Love refuses to do either. It causes a man not to think more highly of himself than he ought to think, but to think soberly (Romans 12:3). These precepts are much minded: Romans 12:10: "Be kindly affectioned one to another, with brotherly love, in honor preferring one another." And Philippians 2:3: "Let each esteem others better than themselves." And as love hinders the heart from being puffed up, so it hinders the tongue from vaunting itself or debasing another. It will not defame or disparage others, as if its own reputation were to be built upon the ruin of theirs. Now this kind of temper is very subservient to the Church's interest; for while Christians are thus low in their own eyes, and are ready both in word and deed to honor and encourage one another, great grace, a shining luster, is upon them all. And God Himself delights in them to make them flourish and increase.

(4) Love does not behave itself unseemly. What is more unseemly than a lofty look or a haughty carriage—as if others were not good enough to unloose the latches of our shoes! But love banishes pride and scornfulness, and makes us humble in our conduct, which is the most seemly behavior in the world. The Greek word signifies any unseemly behavior.

So love studies exactness of carriage, that religion may be the more commended unto all. When professors do that which is unseemly, the Church and religion suffer by it; but a conduct without rebuke, which manifests a love both for God and man, is the way to win many a man to God who before was estranged from Him. An unseemly behavior opens many a mouth against the gospel, creates new prejudices, and confirms the world in their natural enmity against it. But a seemly behavior makes religion amiable; well-doing puts ill tongues to silence, and forces them to give glory to God. 1 Peter 2:12: "Having your conversation honest among the Gentiles, that whereas they speak against you as evildoers, they may by your good works, which they shall behold, glorify God in the day of visitation."

(5) Love seeks not her own, and consequently inclines us to edify and seek the good of others. The Apostle's meaning is not that love causes us to cast off all care and regard of ourselves, but only that which is immoderate, and which, proceeding from a blind self-love, makes us disregard what becomes of others. Christ Himself is a pattern of love in this respect, and love follows Him. He was humbled that we might be exalted. He was condemned that we might be justified. He became poor that we, through His poverty, might be rich. He was made a curse that we might receive the blessing, even live forevermore. Love will make a Christian seek the welfare, the reputation, and especially the salvation of another. Nay, charity will prevail with us to suffer reproach, loss, imprisonment, nay, death itself, when God calls us to it for the Church's good. 1 John 3:16: "Hereby perceive we the love of God, because He laid down His life for us; and we ought to lay down our lives for the brethren." And the apostle says in Colossians 1:24: "I now rejoice in my sufferings for you, and fill up that which is behind of the afflictions of Christ in my flesh, for His

body's sake, which is the Church." Hence it is apparent, says
Calvin, that true charity is not in us by nature, but a grace
from above, really of divine origin.

(6) Love is not easily provoked. Before it was said that
love suffers long, but here something further is intimated:
that though the cause and occasion are very great, yet love is
not ready to be incensed. I grant that, notwithstanding love, a
Christian may be angry at sin; but love makes him fly from
causeless, sinful anger. The Scripture prohibitions are very
strict and severe. Ecclesiastes 7:9: "Be not hasty in thy spirit to
be angry; for anger resteth in the bosom of fools." Psalm 37:8:
"Cease from anger and forsake wrath; fret not thyself in any
wise to do evil." Anger and wrath, what harm has it done in
the Christian world! What rents, what divisions has it made!
Bitter fruit has grown from this root of bitterness. The wrath
of man works not the righteousness of God, nor His Church's
good. And therefore love, which moderates anger and morti-
fies what is sinful and hurtful in it, must do the Church a
kindness. Alas! poor England! and pitiable church in it! How
many parties are there, and how high their exasperations! But
their fury one against another is a perfect frenzy, which has a
certain and speedy tendency unto universal destruction. Want
of love is one of the clearest demonstrations that there is want
of wisdom.

(7) Love thinks no evil. It is not apt to impute evil to
another, but to construe the words and actions of others in
the best sense which they can bear. It is very far from imagin-
ing and contriving evil and mischief against another. To ruin
men's estates, to blast their names, to wound their consciences, to rid the world of them—these are none of love's
contrivances. And as love carries on no evil designs, so it is not
suspicious that others do. These suspicions are very bad, for if
the mind is full of them it will be apt to meditate revenge

upon barely fancied and supposed injuries, though the
Christian religion forbids avenging even real ones. Want of
love makes us imagine that others have contrivances against
us to undermine our interest and repute, and to do us some
great harm, when indeed just the contrary may be true. And
when we think so ill of them, our carriage towards them may
be as ill as our thoughts. But love is too full of candor to give
way to groundless jealousies. And if this candor did but more
prevail, how would edification be promoted! Suspicions keep
the several parties that are among us at a greater distance.
Difference in opinions creates the distance; suspicions widen
it. Several dissenters are apt to suspect Episcopal men inclined to popery. Divers Episcopal men are apt to think that if
ever popery comes in it will be brought in upon the back of
the Puritans. Different parties are all full of jealousies, as if
they were all false unto and intended to ruin utterly one another, and as if each one wanted only to advance themselves.
Now these suspicions, unless there is most apparent ground
for them, should be abandoned. Love will not cherish them,
for they weaken the Protestant religion, and divide the
Church against itself.

    (8) Love rejoices not in iniquity, but rejoices in the
truth. Though our neighbor is to be loved, yet we are not to
love his iniquity, but to endeavor by prayer to God, by reproofs and entreaties, and in other ways to reclaim him from
his evil and destructive way. Leviticus 19:17: "Thou shalt not
hate thy brother in thine heart, but shalt in any wise rebuke
thy neighbor, and not suffer sin to lie upon him." And though
our neighbor has shown himself an enemy to us, and later
falls into some scandalous iniquity whereby he is damaged
and disgraced, love will hinder us from being secretly glad of
it. Nay, it will make us really pity him and mourn for him.
What Solomon says in Proverbs 24:17 is much to our present

purpose: "Rejoice not when thine enemy falleth, neither let thy heart be glad when he stumbleth." To rejoice in the sins of others, how hellish is it! This is so far from edifying that it makes a man exactly resemble the evil one who is the Church's great destroyer. This very bad temper, how it prevails at this day among many persons of different persuasions! When they hear of the scandalous falls of others who are not of their way, they are puffed up, as the Corinthians were, and are too pleased (1 Corinthians 5:2). They hope that the reputation of their party will be advanced by the exclamation that is made against those of another party. And hereby they show that they value their own reputation above the salvation of a soul, the honor of God Himself, and the general credit of Christianity. But where persons are thus glad at the scandalous sins of others, there is certainly a most scandalous lack of charity, which shows itself in proclaiming on the housetops what love should make them cover.

Love rejoices not in iniquity, but it rejoices in the truth, and therefore is truly for edification. "Truth" may be meant by a Hebraism for true goodness, for sincere righteousness, as the antithesis in the words manifests; or truth may refer to the reality of love itself. Love rejoices in the truth because it is an enemy to shows and dissimulation.

I might also add another gloss: we must not love any man or party so as to reject truth, but the truth must be owned with gladness on whichever side or wherever it is found. A philosopher said, "Socrates is my friend, and so is Plato, but truth is more my friend than either."

(9) Love is for the Church's edification, for it hopes and believes all things. It believes the best of others until that which is bad is so visible and apparent that if it does not believe it must be blind. Though one who is truly charitable is unwilling to be imposed upon, yet of the two he rather

chooses to be deceived through his candor and facility than to wrong his brother by a sinister suspicion. And where love for the present cannot believe, yet it will hope. If it sees others to be never so bad, yet it hopes they may come to a better mind, and how earnestly does it pray for their amendment! The Greek tragedian Euripides tells us, "He is the best man who hopes always." The Roman dictator Fabius Maximus did a great kindness to the Commonwealth, almost ruined by Hannibal, in that he did not quite despair in Rome's extremity. Love for the Church will hinder us from giving over all as lost; and hope, being kept alive that the Church in time may become more pure and more united, will put vigor into our endeavors to promote the Church's union and holiness.

(10) Love edifies, for it bears and endures all things. It bears the greatest injuries from the world, and yet wishes the world well; and it endures unkindness from brethren, still remaining kind to them. It is not transported by the fancied intolerableness of any injury so as to render evil for evil; rather it minds the apostle's words in 1 Thessalonians 5:15: "See that none render evil for evil unto any man, but ever follow that which is good, both among yourselves and towards all men."

O love! How much want is there of you in the Church of Christ! And how much does the Church feel for this want! It groans, it languishes, it dies daily because of your absence. Return, O love, return! Repair breaches, restore paths to dwell in, edify the old ways and places, and raise up the foundations of many generations, for after all the most politic contrivances, you will be found the master-builder.

Chapter 7

The Vanity of Excuses for the Want of Love

Having done with the reasons which demonstrate that love is for the Church's edification, I will show, in the fourth place, the vanity of those excuses that are made for the want of love.

1. Some say they are bound to contend earnestly for the faith, and therefore mildness and love in this case are but urged unseasonably—strive they ought, and strive they will.

I answer that sincere Protestants of all persuasions agree in the same faith, and their disagreeing among themselves is the way not to uphold that faith, but to destroy it. The controversies between them are about circumstantials and external modes of worship. They all own the same doctrine of the gospel in opposition to the corruptions and heresies of Rome. That is a bad contention which excludes love. He who believes the gospel of Christ to be the gospel of peace cannot but follow after peace. How well do faith and love agree! Both together make the breastplate of a Christian (1 Thessalonians 5:8), whereby his heart is armed and secured.

2. Others say they will not halt between two opinions. They will follow God and not Baal; they are for Christ and not Antichrist, and are resolved to have no charity for the Beast's worshippers, nor any communion with them.

I answer, do not call that idolatry and antichristianism which Christ calls not by such a name. To charge all conformists with idolatry is a heavy charge, as bold as heavy, and as unreasonable and uncharitable as either. I am sure the martyrs in Queen Mary's days, though conformists, were enabled to suffer the rage of Rome, and loved not their lives unto death that they might bear their testimony against the idolatry of Antichrist. Those who affirm a form of prayer to be a spiritual image, and consequently a breach of the second commandment, seem to me to display a greater strength of fancy than of judgment. I grant that the second commandment forbids the worship of the true God by a false medium or means, and such a false means is an image, for by this means the glory of the incorruptible God is changed into the similitude of a corruptible creature, before which we are forbidden to fall down and worship. So the medium or means forbidden in this law is an object as well as a means. Now those who are most for forms of prayer will deny them to be the objects of their worship; their worship is directed to God alone, and only in the name of Christ the Mediator. That reverend author who asserts a form of prayer to be an image forbidden in the second commandment yet grants that a Christian man, whether a minister or one of private place, may by the gift of prayer which he has received compile to himself a set form of prayer, and may use the same for his prayer whether in public or in private according to his place. But if a form were indeed forbidden, by no means should a man make such a form of prayer for himself.

Further, let me add that all who cry out against antichristianism should beware of uncharitableness, which is a great part of it. Rome is full of cruelty and censures, and condemns all who are not of her way. She affirms that it is impossible that they should be saved. Those in whom Christian love most abounds, I am sure, have come furthest out of Babylon, and are most likely to hinder a return there. What animosities and divisions will do, I wish that time may not too soon manifest.

3. Others plead that they are for a thorough reformation, and the purging of all impurities out of the Church of Christ;

and they cannot endure such as do things by halves only.

I answer that 'tis the glory of the Protestant churches that they are Reformed ones; and none of them are so pure but reformation may be advanced to a higher degree. The compilers of the Common Prayer in the Commination [a part of the liturgy which consisted of a recital of Divine threatenings against sinners] acknowledge that in the primitive church there was a godly discipline which is wanting among us, and they wish that it may be restored. So the need for reformation in discipline is here plainly confessed, and the thing is desired. But a reformation is properly to be sought after, no man using unwarrantable means, nor transgressing the bounds of his vocation.

And while we are talking against impurity in administrations (which the more exactly according to the Word of God, the purer; and the purer the better and more effectual), let us not overlook some of the worst impurities of all. Pride, envy, hatred, and wrath are the impurities of the devil himself. Other sins may have more of the brute or the child, but these have more of Beelzebub. Till you are reconciled to your brother, think not that your offering will be accepted (Matthew 5:24). While the heart is full of bitterness, self-conceit, and strife, do not imagine that you can be a pure worshipper.

4. Others say, "What, shall we love a company of apostates, who are for returning to the onions and garlic of Egypt, and will receive the mark of the Beast itself?"

I answer that the Scripture should be studied and understood, or else it may easily be misapplied. 'Twould better become men to prove a thing to be solidly antichristian than loudly and boldly to call it so. Shall he be branded as an apostate who manifests in his whole conduct a fear of God, who loves the Lord Jesus in sincerity, who owns the great fundamental thoughts of the gospel and is willing, if called to it, to seal them with his blood? Shall he, I say, be branded as an apostate because, to give a legal satisfaction and show that he is no papist, he sometimes hears the prayers of the Church and Scriptures read in a known tongue? Certainly the censurer is a greater apostate from love than this man is from truth. Though the good intentions of persons are to be well taken, and whatever of God is in them is to be loved and encouraged, yet this is to be disliked: that differences between Protestants are made to seem greater than they are. It does not argue a healing spirit to call everything we dislike Egyptian and Babylonish. This uncharitable censuring, if it is not the mark of the Beast, 'tis the mark of one as bad. You know who is called "the accuser of the brethren."

5. Others say that many who pretend to religion and conscience are schismatic and rebellious, and loving and countenancing them only hardens and encourages them in their pernicious ways, to the prejudice both of Church and state.

I answer, particular persons who are culpable should bear the blame. But why should all dissenters be judged rebels? How peaceably have they carried themselves for these many years! How fervently do they pray for the king's life and prosperity! To assassinate his Majesty or the Duke of York they look upon as an action most abominable, and are persuaded that everyone should utterly abhor such a villainous iniquity. They look upon Solomon not as speaking like a politic prince, but as declaring the mind of the Holy Ghost when he says, "My son, fear thou the Lord and the King, and meddle not with them that are given to change" (Proverbs 24:21). They are sensible that the false teachers in the latter days have this character: that they despise government, that "They are presumptuous and self-willed, and are not afraid to speak evil of dignities" (2 Peter 2:10). Let those who are full of bitter invectives against dissenters, as if they were enemies to government, consider what the Assembly of Divines at Westminster declared (and the Congregational Divines at the Savoy said the same) in the Confession of Faith, in the chapter entitled "Of the Civil Magistrate": "It is the duty of people to pray for magistrates, to honor their persons, to pay them tribute and other dues, to obey their lawful commands, and to be subject to their authority for conscience sake." Infidelity or difference in religion "does not make void the magistrate's just and legal authority, nor free the people from their due obedience to him, from which ecclesiastical persons are not exempted; much less hath the Pope any power or jurisdiction over them in their dominions, or over any of their people, and least of all to deprive them of their dominions or lives, if he shall judge them to be heretics, or upon any other pretense whatsoever."

And as for the charge of schism, the dissenters wish there were no such thing in the churches of Christ; that terms of communion might be only scriptural, and that all occasions of division might be taken away. They pray for the peace of Jerusalem, and that she may have more true lovers, and that all may prosper who love her.

Application

I come finally to the application.

USE 1: of information. If love is for the Church's edification, then:

1. Hence we may be informed that hatred, variance, emulations, wraths, strifes, and such works of the flesh tend to the Church's ruin. They who harbor such sins as these, and are not concerned about the mortification of them, are frantic Christians who cast firebrands, arrows, and death, doing

much mischief to others, but most to themselves.

2. No wonder that Satan, who labors to destroy churches, endeavors to kill love. He is the envious one who sows ill weeds; he is the father of lies and errors; he knows error tends to division; he sets an edge on the passions of men, and makes them more sharp and keen; he is the grand incendiary in churches, setting all in a flame, and he hopes this flame will consume all before it, nay, burn at last to the lowest hell.

3. Those principles are truest and best that tend to beget and increase love. The Church of Christ is little beholden to those who are of narrow principles, who mind only a part, but not the whole. The Apostle blamed the Corinthians for being of such a narrow spirit in 1 Corinthians 1:12: "Now this I say, that every one of you saith, 'I am of Paul,' and 'I of Apollos,' and 'I of Cephas,' " whereas all true believers should reckon themselves one in God and Christ, and consequently should be for one another.

4. Hence we may be informed that love is the more excellent way. Rigor and fury may force men to a dissembled compliance, but love is the way indeed to win them. I don't think it a credit to the Koran that it must be seconded with the knocking argument of an iron mace. The Spanish Inquisition shows the weakness of that religion which cannot stand unless it has the help of such cruelty to support it. Certainly that church which is fullest of love is the truest and wisest, and most likely to be enlarged. The Apostle preferred charity before the faith of miracles, though these miracles mightily confirmed the authority and verity of the gospel; nay, he preferred it before the gift of prophecy, though prophecy was the most edifying of all the gifts of the Spirit (1 Corinthians 14:1). He was indeed a prince among preachers, yet even if he were better than he was, and could speak with the tongue of an angel, he said, "Without charity, I am become as sounding brass,

or a tinkling cymbal"; nay, "If I have not charity, I am nothing" (1 Corinthians 13:1–2).

USE 2: of caution, in several particulars.

1. Take heed of what is contrary to love, as that which is contrary to edification. Unmercifulness, cruelty, rage, revenge, and bitterness are so unsuitable to Christianity that they are against humanity itself. When sinful passion first begins to stir in your heart, quench the spark; for "behold how great a matter a little fire kindles" (James 3:5). What is contrary to love is contrary to your own peace, and may make you a disturber of the Church's peace.

2. Take heed of sinful self-love. This causes perilous times to overtake the Church of Christ. 2 Timothy 3:1–2: "This know also, that in the last days perilous times shall come, for men shall be lovers of their own selves." Self-love turns godliness into a form, argues a want of its power, and makes religion subservient unto base and selfish designs; and hereby the gospel comes to be suspected, atheism grows rampant, and the Church languishes. Self-love will make you unconcerned for the honor of God or for the good of man; it will produce a carelessness in you of others' welfare and hinder you from truly minding your own. He who loves nobody but himself, and matters not what harms befall others, so long as he can escape, is a pest of the world, unfit for Christian or human society. Antiquity has censured that speech as infamous: "If I were dead, no matter if the world were all afire." The self-lover is of the same temper: if he can but keep what he has and sleep in a whole skin, he is not at all affected with others' calamities and afflictions.

3. Take heed of scandalizing any. 'Tis the great work of Satan to cause scandals and offenses; and he shows the depth of his subtlety and malice in the management of this pernicious engine. He represents God as too rigorous in His com-

mands and Christ as too much thwarting the glorying of the
flesh. He represents self-denial and the cross as unreasonable
and intolerable; and all this is that man may be offended, and
his conversion to God and faith in Jesus may be hindered.
Our Lord and Savior, who is the great lover of souls, saw the
mischief of scandal, and spoke much to prevent it. He pronounced the woeful misery of the world because of offenses;
but He especially bound and fixed the woe upon "that man by
whom the offense cometh" (Matthew 18:7). After reading
this, I think every man's heart should ache, and he should cry
out, as every one of the disciples did in another case, "Lord, is
it I? Am I the man that Thou sayest 'woe' unto? Does the offense come by me?" 'Tis our duty to love others, but to scandalize them is to be greatly injurious to them; and that's not
an act, a sign of love. There is much talk of scandal, and there
is much more scandal than is talked of. 'Tis a sore evil that
spits its venom every way. It strikes at Jews, at Gentiles, and at
the Church of God. Therefore the Apostle cautions us against
giving offense to any of these (1 Corinthians 10:32). True love
of our neighbor will make us avoid scandal as carefully as a
mariner would a dangerous rock that may cause a shipwreck.
Here I shall lay down some positions concerning scandal that
you may have the truer notion of it, and may flee from it, and
the woe pronounced upon it.

(1) Every displeasing of another is not scandal. 'Tis
one thing to offend a man, and another thing to make him
offend. Barely to displease and grieve another is not to scandalize him; for, if it were, then those professors who are most
ignorant and peevish must be perpetually humored. They
must have their wills or else they will be angry and grieved;
and the weakest (as one observes) must bear sway in the
Church, which they are very unfit to do. And then the
strongest, even pastors themselves, would have to be subject

to them; for they are hugely troubled if they are in the least crossed. Besides, professors are of different minds: some may be angry and grieved at my doing of a thing, others as much displeased and troubled at my not doing it. Now, if barely to offend another were scandal, in this case both scandal and the woe belonging to it might be impossible to avoid. A man may be offended because I am not of his mind, because of my peaceable temper, because I think not that stiffness and strangeness is the way to unity, but mutual yielding and condescension, "forbearing one another in love" (Ephesians 4:2), receiving one another, as Christ has received both the one and the other. Here indeed I may be said to displease, but scandal cannot be laid to my charge.

(2) Scandal is a putting a stumbling block, or an occasion of falling into sin, in another's way. This is the Apostle's definition of scandal. And withal he cautions against Christians judging and censuring one another. Romans 14:13: "Let us not therefore (though of different sentiments and practices) judge one another any more; but judge this rather, that no man put a stumbling block or an occasion to fall in his brother's way." When professors of religion are loose in their lives, and hereby not only confirm the world in their resolution to be unjust, proud, covetous, prodigal of time, and filthy still, but also convey into the hearts of other professors that such strictness as the Scripture requires is needless, and that men may be saved without such circumspect walking—here is scandal with a witness, and 'twill be with a vengeance. And as blinding and stupefying the conscience of another is scandal, so the wounding of the weak conscience of another by drawing him to that which he doubts whether it is lawful is scandal likewise. Love there should make us very tender. Those who are for rigorous imposing upon others should consider what the Apostle said in 1 Corinthians 8:12: "But when ye sin so

against the brethren, and wound their weak conscience, ye sin
against Christ."

(3) Examples of the best are not to be followed with a
doubting conscience. Every man must be fully persuaded in
his own mind concerning the lawfulness of a thing before he
does it; for whatsoever is not of faith is sin, and he who doubts
is damned if he eats (Romans 14:5, 23). I grant that the word
for "doubts" may be translated "puts a difference": "He who
puts a difference between meats, and so eats against his conscience, is damned." But if you consider what follows
("because he eats not of faith"), you see that it is rightly rendered "doubts," for doubting is opposed to faith as well as doing that which undoubtedly is judged unlawful. Thus we find
our Lord making an opposition between doubting and faith.
And the same word is used to express this doubting. Mark
11:23: "Whosoever shall say unto this mountain, 'Be thou removed, and cast into the sea,' and shall not doubt in his
heart, but shall believe that these things which he saith shall
come to pass, he shall have whatsoever he saith." Certainly, as
nothing is to be done against conscience, so nothing with a
doubting conscience; for he who does a thing doubting cannot do that thing in faith.

We should not urge others to follow our example, nor to
do as we do, till they are fully satisfied as we are; nay, we
should press the contrary lest we wound their weak consciences. Romans 14:15: "If thy brother be grieved with thy
meat, now walkest thou not charitably; destroy not him with
thy meat, for whom Christ died." By "grieved" cannot be understood "sorrowed" because another does that which the
brother thinks sinful; for such sorrow will not destroy the
brother. But being grieved implies having one's conscience
wounded, and one's peace broken, by following the example
of another with a doubting mind. The apostle exhorts all to

have faith concerning the lawfulness of a thing before they do it; he cautions against judging and despising one another, though some could do what others could not. And this is the way to prevent scandal, which is so great a piece of uncharitableness. But here I must add that groundless doubts are signs of weakness, and he is a happy man who gets above them; and information that leads to this happiness is very desirable.

(4) Pleasing another so as to occasion his sinning is scandal. The Apostle Peter was a tempter to Christ when he thought to please Him and prevent His suffering; but Christ repelled the temptation presently and rebuked Peter sharply: "Get thee behind Me, Satan, thou art My scandal; thou savorest not the things that be of God, but those things which be of men" (Matthew 16:22–23). The same Apostle (as one observes) scandalized the Jews by pleasing them. For fear of offending the weak Judaizing Christians, he separated from familiar communion with the Gentiles, by which he laid a stumbling block before them to harden them in the sinful opinion of separation. A dangerous scandal it was, whereby Barnabas himself was carried away. Love will make us "please our neighbor for his good to edification" (Romans 15:2). But to please him by doing as he does, saying as he says, and so to harden him in his too-high thoughts of himself, in his error and uncharitableness, in his dividing principles, which have a tendency to hinder the lasting settlement and peace of any church in the world—I say, thus to please him is to scandalize him by not crossing and offending him. Meekly and faithfully instructing him, though it angers him, would be a true expression of love toward him.

(5) In shunning scandal, special regard must be had to the weak who are in greatest danger. He who is weak falls more easily; and therefore stumbling blocks should not be laid, but removed out of his way. Those who suppose them-

selves higher than others in light and grace should be the more condescending to those whom they think much below themselves, and should bear with their infirmities. "We then that are strong ought to bear the infirmities of the weak, and not to please ourselves" (Romans 15:1). Those who differ from us in judgment have precious souls as well as those of our own way; therefore we must take heed of scandalizing them, especially if they are very numerous. We should be wary how we utterly disown a vast body of Christians, as if they were a company of heathen men and publicans. This will confirm them in considering their exasperations and severities against us to be highly reasonable, and they will so fix their eyes upon that in us which we cannot justify that they will the less regard what we speak against those things which may strongly be proven to need a reformation. The more general a scandal is, the more fatal are the effects of it, and the more it proves detrimental to the Church of God.

(6) All should pray against proneness to be offended. Others' actions should not make us more likely to stumble and fall. As the providence of God towards us, though at present never so dark and intricate and unaccountable, should not make us weary of Him, or of His service, because He is a Lord most gracious, and His service is really the best beyond all comparison, so neither should the carriage of men, though never so strange and odd and unexpected, occasion our sinning, nor discourage us in well-doing. Upright men may be astonished at the dispensations of divine providence; they may be amazed to see the world so full of wickedness, and to behold faith failing, love dying, and practical religion so much ceasing in the Church of Christ— yet "they stir up themselves against the hypocrites"; they get over the stumbling blocks that are laid before them; "they hold on their way and wax stronger and stronger" (Job 17:

8–9). Foolish men who are glad of scandal! who run eagerly up and down inquiring, "Who will show us anything that may offend us?" They rejoice at any plea for a sinful course, and greedily catch at anything that may prejudice them against others who are not of their way; nay, they are forward to suck in prejudices against the ministry, ordinances, and the gospel of Jesus Christ. A man who is swift to hear what may scandalize him, who is joyful upon occasions that make him angry and uncharitable, or give him any other way to sin, is like one who in a time of war voluntarily runs upon the sword's point or up to the cannon's mouth, or like one who, in a time of pestilence, does not strive to avoid, but to catch the contagion. A man who should thus be fond of plague or sword you would judge frantic, and he is in a worse sense frantic who is fond of scandal. That's the third caution: take heed of scandalizing any.

4. Take heed of an unbridled tongue. How mighty a hindrance of love has this little member been! Both Church and state have felt the smarting and dangerous wounds, which a lawless tongue has given. The tongue of a serpent, of a viper, the tongue that is all sting and carries poison and death in it, is nothing near so hurtful as the tongue of a liar, of a slanderer. The apostle plainly intimates, and the prophet had done it long before, that the sins of the tongue are the great cause of the badness of the times. 1 Peter 3:10–11: "He that will love life and see good days, let him refrain his tongue from evil, and his lips that they speak no guile; let him eschew evil and do good; let him seek peace and pursue it."

Four things are observable in these words:
(1) An evil tongue is the disturber of peace.
(2) It is a great indication of guile and hypocrisy.
(3) It very often shortens the life.
(4) It is a grand impediment to our seeing good days.

'Tis a vain thing to expect that times should grow better when tongues daily grow worse and worse, and when neither Scripture, reason, nor conscience can keep them to the words of truth and soberness.

When there is so much evil in the tongue, how little of love, how little of good can there be in the heart! Would you have the Church of Christ edified? Let not your tongues wound any of her members, though of a different persuasion from you. Do you love your neighbors as yourselves? Be as backward to speak evil of your neighbors as of yourselves. What our Lord speaks concerning doing may be applied to saying: "Whatsoever ye would that men should say concerning you, say you even so of them." He who knew what was in man tells us, "Out of the abundance of the heart the mouth speaks" (Matthew 12:34). Bitterness in the language argues a root of bitterness within, which the sooner it is plucked up the better.

Take heed of speaking lies to the prejudice of others. Satan the accuser has hardly a more exact picture in this world than a malicious liar. Invent not lies; believe not lies; report not lies. He who spreads a lie to his brother's harm is a hater of his brother; he may talk of love, but is he a stranger to it. Proverbs 26:28: "A lying tongue hateth those that are afflicted by it, and a flattering mouth worketh ruin." Spreading slander is a sign of hatred. Nay, you are not to speak truth with an evil design; clamor and railing at the faults of others make you faulty as well as they. It would be well if, instead of public defamations, there were more friendly, brotherly, and private admonitions. That injunction of Christ, "Tell thy brother his fault between thee and him alone; if he hear thee, thou hast gained thy brother" (Matthew 18:15), is neglected at this day as if it were not in the Bible.

Be not forward to pronounce judgment rashly concerning

others. Christ the Judge says to Christians, "Judge not" (Matthew 7:1). You who speak so much of standing up for the kingly office of Christ, do not usurp His place and office by becoming judges of your brethren; do not cast that great command of this King of kings, to love one another behind your backs.

Avoid partiality in speaking of others. If you extenuate greater crimes in those of your own party, and endeavor to conceal them, and aggravate lesser things in those of another party and blaze them abroad, you respect persons and are "convinced of the law as transgressors" (James 2:9). And as far as there is partiality, so far there is hypocrisy (James 3:17).

O tongues of professors! How long will it be ere you are quiet? How long shall your breath be like the east wind, blasting all about you? When shall all your words be agreeable to the Word of God? When shall your lips feed many and hurt none? Your reproachful, backbiting, railing language, your lies and falsehoods have been your sin and shame, and the shame of religion. Repentance and amendment are absolutely necessary, else salvation still will stand at a distance. Isaiah 63:8: "For He said, 'Surely they are My people, children that will not lie'; so He was their Savior."

USE 3: of exhortation to abound in love, which is so much for the Church's edification. My exhortation I second with these arguments:

1. God is love. His love is inconceivably great towards His whole Church, and every true member of it. There is not the meanest or most mistaking Christian in the world but, if he is sincere, God sets His love and a high price upon him. Ungodly men are but like common stones, but believers are God's jewels, His peculiar treasure above all people (Exodus 19:5). And if God thus loves them all, surely they ought to love one another (1 John 4:11). They who dwell in love dwell

in God. Now to dwell in God is to dwell safely, for He is the Rock of Ages; and in Him mercy, grace, light, peace and joy are to be found.

2. Christ the Head is full of love for all the members. Among these, therefore, there should be a most ardent affection one for another, and a great and sweet agreement. "Comprehend with all saints what is the breadth, and length, and depth, and height, and know the love of Christ which passeth knowledge" (Ephesians 3:18–19). And how will you be able to slander or injure, or be bitter against, any whom Christ loves with a love that passes all understanding?

3. Love is preferred before faith and hope. 1 Corinthians 13:13: "And now abideth faith, hope, and charity, but the greatest of these is charity." Faith and hope cease when we come to see and enjoy; but love never fails or ends. Faith receives and hope expects; but love gives the heart of God, and for His sake it gives liberally to its neighbor. Love is the bond of perfectness (Colossians 3:14). Love ties all other virtues together and makes them more perfect and acceptable; it unites the members of the Church together, which Church is the world's perfection. Psalm 50:2: "Out of Zion, the perfection of beauty, God hath shined."

4. Love is a debt. Romans 13:8: "Owe no man anything, but to love one another." You are not just to your neighbor unless you love him, and love to show mercy to him. He who loves not another defrauds him of what is due to him; nay, he is not only a thief but a murderer. 1 John 3:15: "Whosoever hateth his brother is a murderer, and ye know that no murderer hath eternal life abiding in him." And if he who lacks love is a murderer, 'tis less to say that he is a schismatic; but he may truly be called the greatest schismatic who is most void of love. Heresy is opposed to faith, and schism to charity. And if so, then they are furtherest from schism who are fullest of

love; and they are most schismatic who are fullest of bitterness and rancor against their brethren.

5. The greater your love is, and the more universal it is, it makes you the more complete a communicator of good, the more universal a blessing. The Church is beholden to you, and so is the world. God Himself is pleased to see your charity so diffusive and active; and your labor of love shall not be forgotten, shall not miss of a reward.

USE 4: direction how love may be revived and increased.

1. Observe the great defects of love in you, and be very much ashamed and abased before God. How few of your actions and speeches have savored of love! What workings have there been in your hearts contrary to it! Judge not want of love a small offense, since 'tis so much called for in both law and gospel.

2. Seriously lay to heart how much Christ Himself is concerned in and for all His members, though their opinions may be different from yours. This good Shepherd loves all His flock, and He gave His life as a ransom for every one of them. Backbite not, discourage not, persecute not, and especially destroy not anyone for whom Christ died (1 Corinthians 8:11). Every particular believer should love the universal Church, and should have an interest in the universal Church's love.

3. Search the Scriptures that your light may be increased. The more true knowledge, the more unity (Ephesians 4:13). All sincere hearts have a strong disposition to agree together in the truths of God once they are revealed to them. Pray against errors; for as errors are contrary to truth (which in all its parts agrees with itself), so they often contradict one another, and naturally tend to make divisions.

4. Be very humble and self-denying. There must be great yielding on all sides, putting up with many things, or love will

not be revived. Humility of mind and meekness are the companions of charity, and cherish it exceedingly. Colossians 3:12–14: "Put on, as the elect of God, bowels of mercies, kindness, humbleness of mind, meekness, long-suffering; forbearing one another, and forgiving one another, if any man have a quarrel against any. Even as Christ forgave you, so also do ye; and above all these things put on charity." Abhor pride, which is the cause of contention. That is good counsel which I find in those *Rabbinical Rhythms*, which if followed would increase love.

> Let wisdom above all possessions be;
> Before preferment choose humility.
> Every ill property be sure to depress,
> But principally stiff tenaciousness.

5. Mark those who cause divisions and offenses, and avoid them. They who agree in doctrine, and in the main things of Christianity, should not easily be divided. They should think more of those things wherein they agree than of those wherein they differ. And be sure to deafen your ears to talebearers, whose business is to destroy love and sow discord. The words of a talebearer are as wounds; and how deep do they go! "Where no wood is, the fire goeth out; and where there is no talebearer, the strife ceaseth" (Proverbs 26:20).

6. Let this be your frequent petition, that you may be taught of God to love one another. Pray that the Word, which commands love, may be more deeply engraved in your hearts, and rule there at all times; and that all exasperating thoughts and surmises, all unruly passions which are contrary to love, as enemies to you, to the Church, to God Himself, may be brought into captivity unto Christ, the Prince of Peace.

USE 5: of consolation to the distracted, drooping, desponding Church of Christ, and all the sincere members of it. The grounds of comfort are these:

1. The Church of Christ shall be upheld, notwithstanding all her divisions. What heats, what heresies there were in the primitive times! If one reads the *Catalogue of Errors* in Epiphanius and St. Augustine, which men professing Christianity embraced, and what rents these errors made, it will be just matter of wonder that the Church was not torn to pieces by her own members. Satan has been striking at faith and charity; and yet still there is a Church, and when he has done his worst there will still be one.

2. The love of Christ towards His Church is unchangeable. The members may fail in their duty one towards another, but the faithfulness of the Head never fails. His care is constant. He is the same yesterday, today, and forever (Hebrews 13:8). It is said of Jesus in John 13:1 that "having loved His own that were in the world, He loved them to the end." And this love secured them to the end.

3. There will be no want of love in heaven. Though Christians may not fancy to travel in one another's company, yet they are all going toward the same country and place of eternal rest. And once they have come there, they shall rest from sin and contention as well as from trouble and affliction. In that glorious place and state, there will be no error, no culpable ignorance remaining; both light and love will be in their perfection. And because perfect love is there, perfect peace and joy will be there also. Jerusalem above is a city indeed that is strongly founded, for its Builder and Maker is God (Hebrews 11:10), and it will last forever, and is built accordingly. The triumphant saints who inhabit there, how near are they brought unto God, who is all in all! How closely and inseparably are they knit together in love! Paul and

Barnabas will no more fall out, being both in heaven. Luther and Zwingli are perfectly agreed.

When St. Augustine, as he tells us in his *Confessions*, had been discoursing with his mother concerning heaven—the crown, the joys, the peace, the pleasures there—his mother's heart grew warm with sacred fire; and that warmth at length was heightened into a heavenly rapture, making her cry out, "What shall I do here below! How shall I with patience stay in a vale of tears, who have had such a sight of the glory, such a taste of the joys of the New Jerusalem!" Certainly these thoughts should make sincere Christians long to be above; and it should comfort them that it will not be long ere they are above, when they behold the Church on earth so rent and torn by pride and ignorance, and unruly lusts and passions; it should comfort them to remember that among the innumerable company of angels, and all the glorified saints, there is not the least discord, but a complete and everlasting harmony.

Verses and Poems

I have finished my discourse concerning love and the Church's edification. I shall add a few verses which I wrote when I was a prisoner in the Marshalsea. I find that music relieved Saul when the evil spirit came upon him, and composed the spirit of a prophet when it was ruffled and out of order. Perhaps poetry may have an effect of the like nature. The verses are these:

> Now use thy liberty, my mind,
> Who art not in the least confin'd.
> The whole earth over thou may'st go,
> And view the all that it can show.
> And that great all which thou can'st see
> Is not enough to satiate thee.
> From Gades to Ganges thou may'st run,
> (Thy thought's much swifter than the sun)
> And in thy travel nothing spy
> But what is vexing vanity.
> The greedy worldling spares no pains;
> The more he has, the less he gains:
> To profit others does refuse;
> Nay, locks up all from his own use.
> Sensual pleasures mixed be
> With an inward anxiety.
> The brutish part they only please,
> But are the mind's snare and disease.
> Th' ambitious man strives to climb high,
> That he may stand more slippery.
> The glist'ring crowns which monarchs wear

Have less of honor than of care.
Vain world! produce even all thy store,
Thou art indeed a thing but poor.
Nay, heaven's heirs have felt thy rage
In this, as every former Age.
If not by an excessive love
An idol made of, thou dost prove
A Hell, or shambles unto them
Who dare thee with thy all contemn.
The Church is too much like the world,
Into a strange confusion hurl'd,
Envy, and wrath, and pride, and strife,
Embittering this present life.
By all is plain enough expressed;
Arise, depart, here's not thy rest.
Trample on Earth, then take thy flight,
Immortal Soul! Things out of sight,
Above the sun, or any star,
Are worthiest of thy thoughts by far.
Let not thy senses tailors be,
Nor what suits them infatuate thee.
Open thy eyes, behold thy God;
Rise with thy Lord, that thy abode
May be with Him that's Light and Love;
Nay, all in all that are above.
The persecution most fierce
Can no way hinder their converse
With heaven: Though in a dungeon deep
As the Earth's center, Foes should keep
The body close, yet thou art free;
And thy best Friend to visit thee;
The joyful tokens of His love,
Prisons are palaces, do prove;

Nay, paradises of delight,
Although they silly nature fright.
Sorrow is joy, and pain is pleasure;
Disgrace is honor, loss a treasure.
The world when worst, is best of all
To those God does to suffer call.
The New Jerusalem comes down,
Is clearly'st seen when men most frown,
And with the sharpest thorns thee crown.
Take up thy cross, which is thy trial,
And taste the sweets of self-denial.
God is thy Father, and thy rest;
Abide with Him, and thou art blest.

The following poem was more lately composed.

A Welcome to Disesteem

I.
The world's a siren, and its sweetest song
The greatest wrong.
Th' applause of men the prais'd endangereth
Like poisonous breath.
The wings of fame like those of Icarus,
pernicious.
He that ambitious is of estimation,
Shows himself fond of peril and temptation.

II.
In the most of men a change is seen as soon
As him in th' moon.

A word, a look can quench the hottest love,
And anger move.
The fondest friend oft turns the worst of foes,
And fury blows.
Whoso does think to make men always kind,
He may as well attempt to hold the wind.

III.
On mountains high the tempests fiercest are,
And nothing spare.
The tops of loftiest buildings in a town
Are soonest down.
He that's above is envied to death
By those beneath.
Ambition does prove a fatal charm,
And makes a man expose himself to harm.

IV.
Unconstant world! how low should wise men deem
Thy high esteem!
To better bad men, Honor has no force,
Makes good men worse.
Honor is fitly styled the foolish fire
That flies desire;
But fondly follows such as scorn and fly it,
That they may be misled and ruined by it.

V.
What peace and safety is in being low,
The Prudent know.
Christ's Head did fly the circle of a crown
And great renown;
The whole world offered He did refuse,

And meanness choose.
To follow wisdom's pattern can't be folly;
Dishonor's no just ground of melancholy.

VI.
False world! thy ill report I'll not deserve,
It shall me serve.
Thy frowns and slanders shall a kindness do,
Not make me rue.
When friends turn foes, and foes, more foes I see,
It weaneth me
From things below, and kills excessive love,
Where doting my destruction might prove.

VII.
I will the rage of froward men, and spite,
With love requite.
It troubles me to see professors' ire
Burning like fire.
I wish I were all tears to check the flame,
And quench the same.
If wrath shut ears against my ministry,
I will to God for all the louder cry.